Company's Coming

LEARN TO

Craft With Paper

Flower Bloom Tray, page 112

www.companyscoming.com
visit our website

Home Tweet Home, page 26

Learn to Craft With Paper

Copyright © Company's Coming Publishing Limited

First Printing November 2009

Library and Archives Canada Cataloguing in Publication
Learn to craft with paper.
(Company's Coming crafts)
Includes index.
ISBN 978-1-897477-26-7
1. Paper work. 2. Handicraft. I. Title: Craft with paper. II. Series: Company's coming crafts
TT870.L425 2009   745.54   C2009-901763-6

Published by
Company's Coming Publishing Limited
2311-96 Street
Edmonton, Alberta, Canada T6N 1G3
Tel: 780-450-6223   Fax: 780-450-1857
www.companyscoming.com

Company's Coming is a registered trademark owned by Company's Coming Publishing Limited

Printed in China

The Company's Coming Story

Jean Paré grew up with an understanding that family, friends and home cooking are the key ingredients for a good life. A mother of four, Jean worked as a professional caterer for 18 years, operating out of her home kitchen. During that time, she came to appreciate quick and easy recipes that call for everyday ingredients. In answer to mounting requests for her recipes, Company's Coming cookbooks were born, and Jean moved on to a new chapter in her career.

Company's Coming founder Jean Paré

Just as Company's Coming continues to promote the tradition of home cooking, the same is now true with crafting. Like good cooking, great craft results depend upon easy-to-follow instructions, readily available materials and enticing photographs of the finished products. Also like cooking, crafting is meant to be enjoyed in the home or cottage. Company's Coming Crafts, then, is a natural extension from the kitchen into the family room or den.

In the beginning, Jean worked from a spare bedroom in her home, located in the small prairie town of Vermilion, Alberta, Canada. The first Company's Coming cookbook, *150 Delicious Squares*, was an immediate bestseller. Today, with well over 150 titles in print, Company's Coming has earned the distinction of publishing Canada's most popular cookbooks. The company continues to gain new supporters by adhering to Jean's "Golden Rule of Cooking"—Never share a recipe you wouldn't use yourself. It's an approach that has worked—millions of times over!

Company's Coming cookbooks are distributed throughout Canada, the United States, Australia and other international English-language markets. French and Spanish language editions have also been published. Sales to date have surpassed 25 million copies with no end in sight. Familiar and trusted in home kitchens around the world, Company's Coming cookbooks are highly regarded both as kitchen workbooks and as family heirlooms.

Because Company's Coming operates a test kitchen and not a craft shop, we've partnered with a major North American craft content publisher to assemble a variety of craft compilations exclusively for us. Our editors have been involved every step of the way. You can see the excellent results for yourself in the book you're holding.

Company's Coming Crafts are for everyone—whether you're a beginner or a seasoned pro. What better gift could you offer than something you've made yourself? In these hectic days, people still enjoy crafting parties; they bring family and friends together in the same way a good meal does. Company's Coming is proud to support crafters with this new creative book series.

We hope you enjoy these easy-to-follow, informative and colourful books, and that they inspire your creativity. So, don't delay—get crafty!

TABLE OF CONTENTS

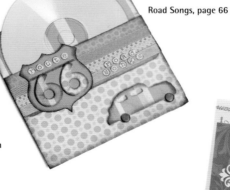

Road Songs, page 66

Cherish Accordion
Book, page 42

Dream Card,
page 24

TABLE OF CONTENTS

Encouragement Key Chains, page 80

Christmas Tree Gift Set, page 120

Fall Patchwork Frame, page 98

Feeling Crafty? Get Creative!

Each 160-page book features easy-to-follow, step-by-step instructions and full-page colour photographs of every project. Whatever your crafting fancy, there's a Company's Coming Creative Series craft book to match!

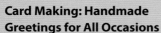

Beading: Beautiful Accessories in Under an Hour

Complement your wardrobe, give your home extra flair or add an extra-special personal touch to gifts with these quick and easy beading projects. Create any one of these special crafts in an hour or less.

Knitting: Easy Fun for Everyone

Take a couple of needles and some yarn and see what beautiful things you can make! Learn how to make fashionable sweaters, comfy knitted blankets, scarves, bags and other knitted crafts with these easy to intermediate knitting patterns.

Card Making: Handmade Greetings for All Occasions

Making your own cards is a fun, creative and inexpensive way of letting someone know you care. Stamp, emboss, quill or layer designs in a creative and unique card with your own personal message for friends or family.

Patchwork Quilting

In this book full of throws, baby quilts, table toppers, wall hangings—and more—you'll find plenty of beautiful projects to try. With the modern fabrics available, and the many practical and decorative applications, patchwork quilting is not just for Grandma!

Crocheting: Easy Blankets, Throws & Wraps

Find projects perfect for decorating your home, for looking great while staying warm or for giving that one-of-a-kind gift. A range of simple but stunning designs make crocheting quick, easy and entertaining.

Sewing: Fun Weekend Projects

Find a wide assortment of easy and attractive projects to help you create practical storage solutions, decorations for any room or just the right gift for that someone special. Create table runners, placemats, baby quilts, pillows and more!

For more information about Company's Coming craft books, visit our website, www.companyscoming.com

FOREWORD

When learning to craft with paper it is essential to become familiar with the basic products that you'll be working with, and it's important to understand the different types of papers and adhesives available in order to achieve the best results with your projects. We'll cover the differences between card stock, vellum, mulberry paper and more. Our handy guide to adhesives will help you determine which adhesive is right for the paper or project that you're creating.

In the first chapter, Learn to Fold Paper, we'll explore some of the basic options for folding paper and define terms like accordion folds and gate folds. Turn a simple project into one with layers and depth by creating mountains and valleys! Gate folds resemble French doors and are widely used in greeting cards and on scrapbook pages as a unique way to conceal journaling.

Learn to Rip Paper will show you one of the easiest ways to add subtle dimension to your paper crafting projects. This is a great paper crafting technique that requires no special tools—just your hands and some paper. Of course, if you're a perfectionist and need the torn edges of your paper to be precise, there are a number of rulers and guides available to help you achieve that.

Only your imagination will limit you when it comes to learning ways to give paper crafting projects a distressed or vintage look. With Learn to Distress Paper, we'll cover some of the basic distressing techniques and tools. This technique has enjoyed wide-spread popularity and it seems that more innovative ways to distress paper are created all the time.

With Learn to Choose Ink for Paper, we'll help you decipher the mystery of ink and answer some common questions among paper crafters. Is the ink acid free and archival quality? Is it fast-drying? What kinds of ink are best suited for use with embossing powders? Which inks work best on hard surfaces such as metal or plastic? Creative minds need to know how to use ink for a variety of paper projects.

Learn to Emboss will teach you ways to incorporate subtle raised designs on paper crafts. We'll explore two of the most common approaches to this versatile technique—wet and dry embossing. One method is achieved with ink and embossing powders and the other with templates and an embossing tool. Both methods are sure to please no matter what your level of crafting expertise is.

And in Learn to Stitch on Paper, you'll discover why stitching is no longer limited to individuals who enjoy sewing or quilting. We will show you how to incorporate delicate hand-stitched or quick machine-stitched embellishments on your next paper craft project for a wonderfully homemade feel.

There's a whole world of options when it comes to crafting with paper—there's no limit to what you can create with a few supplies and some imagination. Dive into any of the projects in the book, or adapt these ideas to add your own personal touches. No matter what you choose, you'll soon find out why so many crafters love working with paper to create a variety of projects. Happy crafting!

THE BASICS OF PAPER CRAFTING

By | Judi Kauffman

Each person's must-have paper list will vary since tastes and interests are so different, but some basic papers are staples, much like sugar, flour and salt in the kitchen cupboard. The extras, those things each of us chooses to spice things up, are what make our scrapbook pages, greeting cards and other projects as unique as we are.

Card stock and paper are a good value. Even the most expensive sheets are bargains when you consider that no scrap need go to waste. Stock up on 8½ x 11-inch and 12 x 12-inch solid, speckled or flannel card stock in a personal palette of six to ten colours, minimum. Begin with neutrals like white glossy, white matte finish, ivory, cream or oatmeal. Add to that several shades of red, green, some pastels, navy and black. Build your stash to include colours that fit the season or the theme of the project you're working on. Keep other colours on hand in smaller quantities, adding orange and brown in the fall, ice blue in winter, and teal, sea foam and celadon in summer.

Buy stacks of your favourites when you find colours you can't live without. When you find papers that are on sale or discontinued, buy plenty and stock up. Chain stores often have specials as low as 6 to 10 cents a sheet to lure customers in the door. Buying in large quantities significantly lowers the price, plus it's a lot of fun to share with friends, spreading the bargain to two or more people. Try choosing interesting finishes like flannel, speckled, linen and laid (striped), as well as the plain smooth or shiny papers.

Love Card, page 22

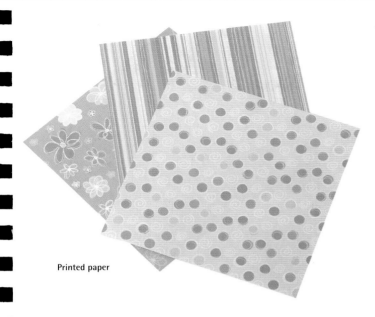

Printed paper

There are two ways to shop for paper: buy for a specific project or simply when you see something that you like. Most of us tend to do both. If you shop with a project in mind, head for the rack where the products you need can be found and buy exactly what you need, or order online. If you're in a store, you can look down the aisles and see what else catches your eye.

Probably the three most important words in paper crafting are as follows: Just in case. The rule is to buy paper that you think you might need, even if you don't yet know why or when you might use it. Paper costs less than lattes or DVDs—indulge yourself. This is one category where the only problem with going overboard is finding space for what you've bought. You can even select sheets purely for inspiration—a paper collection that you enjoy for no reason other than its sheer beauty.

If you do a lot of rubber stamping, buy a sheet or two and test it with your favourite inks, using fine line detailed stamps, bolder graphics and alphabets before investing in a large amount. Tear, cut, emboss and otherwise experiment. The more you know about the papers you own, the more value you will derive from them.

Once you have a good stash of solid colours, head for the printed, patterned and textured sheets. Here's where you have a chance to develop your style and play with something new and different. Buy a transparency sheet or two, some vellum, embossed and imported sheets: handmade exotic papers with texture or smooth-milled mulberry paper. In addition to the standard sizes, there are stacks of paper sold like drawing pads, paper bound into books and single large sheets. You can buy preselected assortments or scrap packs sold by weight too.

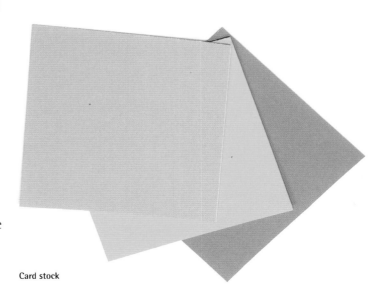

Card stock

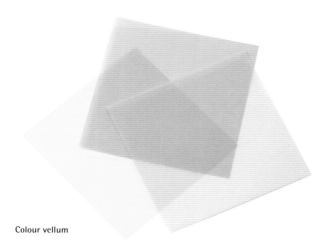

Colour vellum

For ease, speed and so that you don't damage the card stock when you want to access a stack, cut a piece of heavy cardboard about 12 inches long for the bottom of each shelf and use it to pull the stack in and out. Keep the 12 x 12-inch card stock in a tall tower made of storage cubes with shelves. Paper that comes bound in books can be stored just like other kinds of books, spine showing on a shelf, easy to reach. For classes and workshops, transfer what you need to folders and flat boxes and tuck them into a tote. If you are making projects that need to last for generations, look for the words acid- and lignin-free. Be aware that the acid in your hands and the climate in which you work can alter the properties of paper significantly, so do not store your paper, albums or other things you make in a hot attic or wet basement. If projects get handled a lot, even if they start out acid-free, they won't end up that way. That's why sheet protectors are so important for albums.

Texture paper

Of course, most of us buy paper and card stock to use, not to hoard. This means that the minute you have more than a few sheets on hand you also have to organize and remember what you have. Here are some tips for storage.

Keep paper dry and flat, away from humidity and moisture. Choose racks or boxes that fit your space and your style. Try an office supply store mail divider with compartments for 8½ x 11-inch papers and card stock. Each shelf can hold a ream of lightweight paper, about a hundred sheets of heavy card stock. Organize by colour for the solid colour card stock, and keep vellum together, regardless of colour. Group floral patterns together with textures. Metallics could have their own compartment.

Mulberry paper

Interactive scrapbook pages, while exciting and creative, won't last as long as those that aren't touched frequently, especially by small children who might have just finished a jelly sandwich.

Speaking of children, paper is one of the best gifts you can give them. Each time you shop, bring home something especially for them. Help the kids in your life organize a

Patterned vellum paper

work space with supplies that include markers, crayons and age-appropriate scissors.

When children come to visit, have a stack handy that you can point to and say, "Use whatever you want!" Some of it can be small scraps left after die-cutting shapes, or odd bits and pieces, but try to share some of the "good stuff" that you use. Their eyes will light up and their hands will get to work. Hours later, you'll marvel at what they've made—creativity can begin with paper. That's why you should always keep a variety of paper on hand. Just in case you need it! ■

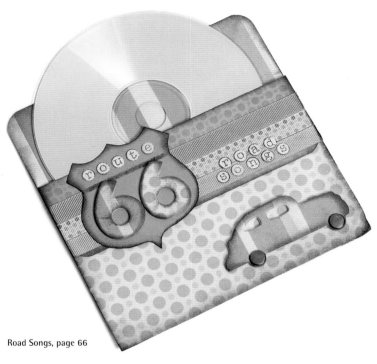

Road Songs, page 66

AN ADHESIVE FOR EVERY STICKY SITUATION

By | Leslie Frederick

Adhesives come under the same umbrella as movie stars, good books and ice cream flavours—everyone has favourites and we are often hard-pressed to explain why.

We just know we like them and we are comfortable with them. Most paper crafters figure out which sticky stuff works best for their favourite projects. But for the novice, or for someone trying a new craft for the first time, the correct adhesive choice can be anything but clear.

In the past, choices in adhesives were limited to white glue (like Elmer's or Aleene's), paste (which someone always had to taste) or rubber cement. Eventually a clever individual invented the glue stick and teachers everywhere breathed a sigh of relief (as did students, who no longer had to spend the better part of the last week of school scrubbing off the layer of glue stuck to the top of their desks).

Over the last few years, adhesive products have multiplied at an astounding speed, sometimes taking over an entire aisle in craft stores. One feels the need for an advanced degree in "glue-ology" before even venturing down that aisle. Have courage! Soon, all the mysteries of those bottles, sticks, tubs and tubes will be solved, and you'll be able to purchase just what you need and have it work the way you desire.

When determining what adhesive you'll need, you want to first consider the surfaces of the items to glue together.

For the sake of simplicity, this article is divided into sections detailing the most popular adhesives so that you can easily find and research the type you need for your project. Some reader favourites may have been left out, but this is simply meant to be a guideline, and not an exhaustive list.

Glues

Most of us are familiar with **glue sticks,** in which the adhesive product has been solidified and is placed in a tube that can be pushed up and out at one end. Some glue sticks come out of the tube in a colour and change to clear as they dry, making it easy to see where the glue has been applied.

Glue pens contain a lightweight liquid glue that goes on wet, and when used wet, is considered permanent once applied. If allowed to dry slightly before adhering, most liquid glues

take on a semi-permanent or repositionable quality so you can move items around before committing to their placement on your project.

Both glue sticks and glue pens are easy to use, travel well and are great for kids. They are inexpensive and available everywhere from discount and grocery stores to office supply and craft stores.

Specialty liquid glues are great for many paper applications, especially when working with articles that require more tack. Several companies make specialty liquids to work for specific needs. In this case, the concept of less is more is often a good rule of thumb. If the project calls for a fine bead of adhesive, look for a liquid with a small, thin nozzle, or find a product that includes different types of nozzles for different applications. If these aren't available, try working from a palette and applying the glue with a toothpick to control the amount of glue that goes on your project. Most liquid glue bottles are as unpredictable as ketchup bottles, and the results to your project can be as disastrous as ketchup on a white T-shirt. New liquid glues on the market are being designed to decrease the wrinkling effect often associated with liquid adhesives. **Zip Dry Paper Glue** from Beacon is a product that specifically addresses that problem. It bonds many different materials to paper without wrinkling the paper. Another new adhesive, **Perfect Glue**, actually draws moisture in the air to help it cure. For those of you in warm climates whose projects fall apart when the humidity rises, give this product a try.

With paper crafts, we most often want to attach one type of paper to another type of paper. Most simple applications of card stock to card stock can

be accomplished with a glue stick or a gel glue that comes in a pen-type applicator. Scrapbookers, on the other hand, are most concerned with adhering photos. The original photo adhesive used, in the majority of early scrapbooks, was either rubber cement or photo corners. Today's scrapbook artists have many more choices available to them.

Photo Adhesives

Photo splits are tiny squares of double-sided adhesive that allow the crafter to place a square at each corner on the back of the photo to adhere the picture in place. The downside of this product is the small tab of paper that is left over from the application. But the advent of new applicators that allow the tab of paper to stick to a carrying sheet means less mess and more success for the user. Many types of applicators are available, so it becomes a simple process of trial and error to decide which type fits your personal style and need.

Photo corners are widely available and come in a variety of different colours, styles and decorative forms. Photo corners are for use on photos that may need to be removed from their album. Older heritage photos can also be adhered with photo corners to preserve the delicate back of the photo. Photo corners in black can enhance the look of heritage albums.

General Adhesives

Adhesive runners make it easy to apply a line of double-sided adhesive to the project without having to touch the project and add the acidity inherent in our skin. Adhesive runners are usually refillable and come in two types, permanent and repositionable. Permanent is just what the name implies, so when using this type of adhesive, be sure of the placement of the element to be adhered. Repositionable adhesives allow you the luxury of moving the element from place to place on your project. Some repositionable adhesives even take the form of lightweight dots of adhesive that can be brushed away with a gum eraser, stiff paintbrush or even your fingers (although that does defeat the purpose of keeping the acidity of your skin from touching the project). Refills are available for most runners, so you may want to choose one that has refills readily available. The refill should be easy to load, as nothing is more frustrating than fighting with an adhesive runner or having to constantly take it back to the store to have it loaded!

Glue spots are dots of glue on a release paper. These are great for numerous purposes, but are primarily used for embellishments such as buttons, charms, fibres and other heavy materials. Glue spots are sometimes available in a dispenser similar to an adhesive runner. The dispenser eliminates the downside of this type of adhesive, which is a long sheet of release paper trailing from your worktable.

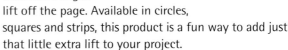

Foam tape comes in a variety of sizes and styles. This product adds dimension to projects by giving elements a slight lift off the page. Available in circles, squares and strips, this product is a fun way to add just that little extra lift to your project.

Specialty Adhesives

Vellum is a material that poses a real dilemma for adhesive manufacturers. The very nature of the product—its translucent quality—means that the adhesive also shows through when placed on the back of the paper. Eyelets and brads became the most viable alternative because no adhesive was required. When adhesive was used, it was most often placed over the entire vellum sheet so that no one area on the vellum was obviously glued down. Xyron machines that apply adhesive to an entire sheet of paper at once became the adhesive of choice for vellum. New adhesives have been developed that work well on vellum, as well as vellums that are self-adhesive.

Embossing tape (or red tape, as it is often referred to as) has become extremely popular with paper artists who favour the use of weighty embellishments or need an adhesive that can be embossed without melting away under heat. The carrier sheet of the tape is red, hence the name. Much like masking tape, embossing tape comes on a circle of cardboard, and many paper artists end up wearing it as a makeshift bracelet while they work so that the adhesive is always handy. You'll need a sharp pair of scissors to cut off the pieces you need, as this tape is too thick to tear easily. Both the weight and the tack of this tape help it hold with a strong bond. It also is a wonderful adhesive when creating pockets on cards or memory pages, keeping the bottom and sides of the pocket securely closed.

Adhesives are one of the paper crafter's most useful tools. After reading this article, you will hopefully feel more confident than ever about choosing the correct adhesive for your next project. ■

ADHESIVE	APPLICATION	PROS	CONS	AVAILABILITY
Glue pens and glue sticks	Paper to paper, lightweight embellishments	Inexpensive, travels well, easy to use	May not have strong enough hold for some applications	Readily available in discount, grocery and office supply stores, as well as scrapbook and rubber stamp stores
Liquid glues (New developments in technology keep this category growing)	Liquid glues (New developments in technology keep this category growing)	Strong bond for specialty uses; look for precision tips for more control	Hard to control, messy	Available in discount stores, rubber stamp and scrapbook stores
Photo splits Photo corners	Photos to scrapbooks	Easy to use, inexpensive, corners allow photos to be removed for copying	When not in dispenser form, leftover tabs can be annoying	Readily available in discount and scrapbook stores
Adhesive runners (new companies are entering this market making products more accessible)	Photos, paper to paper, embellishments	Easy to use, able to cover large area quickly, allows adhesive line to be applied easily	Refills may be difficult to replace	Some runners are more readily available than others, check to see if you can get refills easily for your chosen product
Glue spots	Paper to paper, embellishments	Easy to use, small size	Expense, leftover carrier sheet	Available in discount stores, rubber stamp and scrapbook stores
Foam tape	3-D effects	Allows dimensional feel	Project may become too bulky for page protector or envelope	Available in discount stores, rubber stamp and scrapbook stores
Vellum adhesive	Vellum	Clear application on vellum	Expense, Availability	Available in rubber stamp, scrapbook stores and on the Web
Embossing tape (red tape)	Heavy embellishments, glitter, crystals, embossable products	Strong bond, variety of widths, carrier sheet helps define placement	Expense, availability, must be cut with scissors, leftover carrier sheet	Available in rubber stamp, scrapbook stores and on the Web

LEARN TO FOLD PAPER

Wondering how to give your next paper project that extra-special touch? Try your hand at various paper-folding techniques for a unique look.

By | Julie Ebersole

Many crafters find themselves in the habit of making cards the same way nearly every time by using either a horizontal or vertical fold in the centre. However, breaking away from these traditional methods of folding a card can elevate a project from ordinary to extraordinary, giving it added flair and dimension.

Generally speaking, there are two ways of using folds in card crafting: making folds part of the card's actual construction, and using folds to create a decorative embellishment for your card. We recommend investing in a bone folder. This useful little tool is relatively inexpensive and readily available at most stationery, craft and art supply stores. One end has a dull point, which is used alongside a ruler for creating score lines; the flat edge of the folder is used to press and flatten the fold. While most bone folders are made from plastic, the best are made of real cow bone. A good bone folder helps you make clean, crisp folds, slides smoothly along the paper and will not leave undesirable marks on the project.

Some folds are as simple as turning up the corner of the front panel and securing it with an eyelet or button, or perhaps tying it down with ribbon through a hole punched into it. For added contrast and interest, try stamping or applying a decorative background paper to the corner prior to folding.

A gatefold is a break from the traditional top- or side-folded card. To do this, find the centre point of a panel of card stock and mark it lightly in pencil. Fold the left and right edges of the panel so they meet in the centre, using the pencil mark as a guide. (It helps to imagine this type of fold as a set of French doors.) You can then mount a focal image to the left panel of the gatefold, centring it so that it overlaps the right panel. You can also mount several smaller images, alternating them on the left and right panels, for added impact.

Gatefold sample

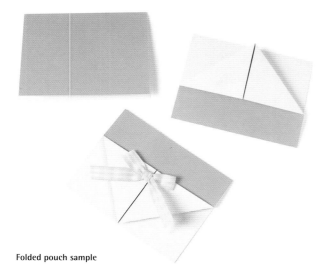

Folded pouch sample

be used to apply the score lines directly to the base card so that it collapses inward when closed, and expands to reveal a message inside as it is opened.

Another interesting card variation is to combine cutting and folding. Start with a standard side-opening card. Open the card and stamp an image in the centre of the inside front panel. Score a line from the top centre of the front panel until it meets the top edge of the stamped image. Finish scoring from the bottom edge of the stamped image down to the bottom of the panel. Use a craft knife with a sharp blade to cut around the right side only of the stamped image, starting and ending at the score lines. Now, carefully crease the front panel, folding it back on itself. The partially cut-out image will appear centred on the card and as one pulls the front panel to the left to open it, the image will appear to pivot slightly from the outside to the inside.

Need a pocket on your card to hold a message or trinket? Fold both corners of a top-folding card upward so they meet. Then punch holes and tie the corners to each other with pretty ribbon, creating a pouch on the front of your card. You can then tuck some crinkled shreds of paper and small goodies inside and your card instantly becomes a greeting and a gift in one!

Try creating a top- and bottom-folding card by scoring and folding the card so that the top overlaps the bottom. Create a unique closure by using a die cut and securing it to the bottom flap of the card so that it will hold the top flap down.

For a card with an interactive nature, try an explosion fold. Typically, this is done by starting with a decorated square of text-weight paper. This sheet is folded and secured inside a card in such a way that when opened, the inside of the card unfolds outward, giving the effect of an explosion. There are also templates available that can

Explosion fold sample

Like the musical instrument for which they are named, accordion cards are pleated—back-and-forth folds that create dimension and excitement. Picture a mountain range with valleys between the peaks—accordion cards use terminology borrowed from the landscape. Folds that extend upward are called "mountain" folds, while those that dip down are "valley" folds.

Diagrams for accordion cards use two different kinds of dotted lines for the two kinds of folds, or two different colours—and it is important to get the mountain and valley folds in the right places.

With a simple card that is folded in half, the scoring and folding is important but not critical. You can always trim a bit if you're off-centre. With accordion cards, however, take your time—careful measuring, scoring and folding spell the difference between a terrific accordion card and a lopsided disaster.

Proportion is a key element in accordion cards. If folds are close together, the effect is akin to a fan. The smaller the card, the closer the folds can be. For example, folds that are spaced at 1-inch intervals work fine for a gift tag, but panels on a traditional card are usually 2 to 4 inches wide.

Folds can be evenly or unevenly spaced, and accordion cards can fold from a centre panel, forming pleated panels both left and right and/or heading in one direction (left to right) only.

All of the elements on an accordion card can be contained within the panels. They can also extend beyond the folds, peeking out when the card is closed, but often revealing more when the card is opened. ■

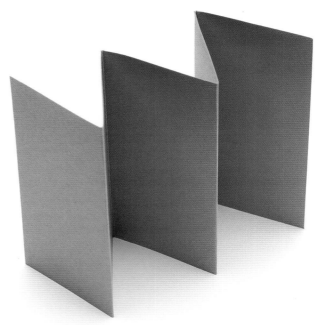

Accordion fold sample

PASTEL EGG ORNAMENTS

Create eye-catching Easter ornaments with coordinating papers and a simple paper-folding technique.

Designs | Lorine Mason

Materials

$2^{7}/_{16}$ x $11^{3}/_{16}$-inch plastic foam eggs
Printed papers: 2 complementary designs/shades of one colour for each ornament
Silver filigree bead cap
$^{1}/_{2}$-inch-wide sheer ribbon in coordinating colours
Straight pins
Paper glue

Instructions

Cut papers into strips 1 inch wide x length of sheet. Cut strips into 2-inch sections. Lay sections pattern side down; referring to Figures 1–3, fold each into a triangle.

Starting at narrow end of egg, pin four triangles, alternating prints, with points meeting on narrow end of egg. Insert pin at each point and each end of each triangle. Paper should conceal plastic foam.

Figure 1

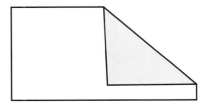

Figure 2

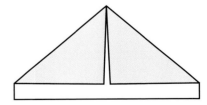

Figure 3

Pastel Egg Ornament

Beginning ¼ inch above point of first triangle, pin a second row of triangles around egg, pinning first triangle in second row between points of two triangles in first row. Conceal pins in first row under triangles in second row.

Continuing in this fashion, work up the egg, covering it in rows of paper triangles. Fold tiny pleats in ends of triangles as needed so they will lie flat.

At top (broad end) of egg, end with a row of four paper triangles with their corners folded under.

For bow, cut strips of ribbon: two 4-inch, two 3-inch, two 2½-inch, two 2-inch and one 1-inch. Overlap ends of each to form loop; push pin through centre of loop, catching ends.

Push pins of 4-inch loops into top (broad end) of egg, crisscrossing loops. Add 3-inch loops, positioning them between the first two. Continue with 2½- and 2-inch loops. At very top, form loop from 1-inch piece of ribbon; push pin through overlapped ends and into top of egg.

Using glue, adhere silver bead cap over pins at bottom (narrow end) of egg. ■

Pastel Egg Ornaments
STYROFOAM® brand plastic foam eggs
from The Dow Chemical Co.; Zip Dry
Paper Glue from Beacon Adhesives Inc.

LOVE CARD

*A heart folded from printed paper creates
the ideal focal point on this romantic card.*

Design | Nancy Billetdeaux

Materials

4½ x 6-inch card with envelope
Solid-colour and printed papers
Text stamps
Purple pigment ink pad
Satin ribbon
Paper glue

Card

Stamp text around edges of card front. Glue a 4½ x 3-inch
piece of solid-colour paper to card front inside stamped
border. Using provided pattern, cut hearts on fold of
printed paper and fold end hearts as indicated. Adhere a
22-inch length of ribbon to wrong side of centre heart.

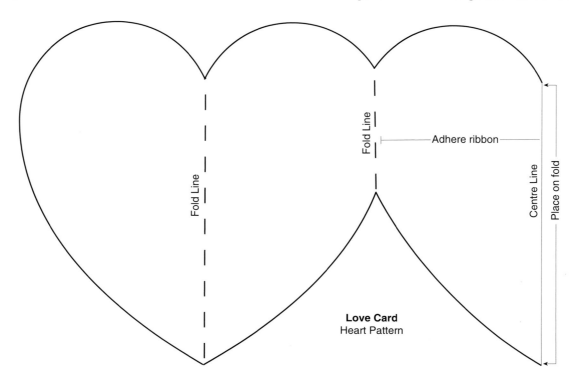

Fold Line

Fold Line

Adhere ribbon

Centre Line

Place on fold

Love Card
Heart Pattern

Adhere centre heart to card front. Stamp message on a 1 x 3⅞-inch piece of solid-colour paper and glue inside heart. Fold in end hearts and tie ribbon in a bow.

Envelope

Referring to photo for placement, cut solid-colour paper to fit envelope flap; cut printed scrapbook paper to fit over solid paper. Glue in place. ■

Love Card
Blank card and envelope, papers, stamps, ink pad and ribbon from Anna Griffin Inc.

DREAM CARD

Embellished with satin ribbons and decorative punches, these beautiful cards will inspire and uplift.

Design | Nancy Billetdeaux

Materials

4½ x 6-inch card with envelope
Card stock
Scrapbook paper
Stamps: text, ornamental frame
Purple pigment ink pad
Satin ribbon
Decorative paper punch
Double-sided tape
Paper glue

Card

Stamp text around edges of card front. Fold a 12 x 3⅛-inch piece of scrapbook paper according to diagram and glue to centre front of card; punch through single layer on each end using decorative punch. Adhere a 24-inch length of ribbon to front of scrapbook paper using double-sided tape. Stamp ornamental frame on scrap of card stock, then stamp text inside frame and cut out; tape frame to inside centre of card.

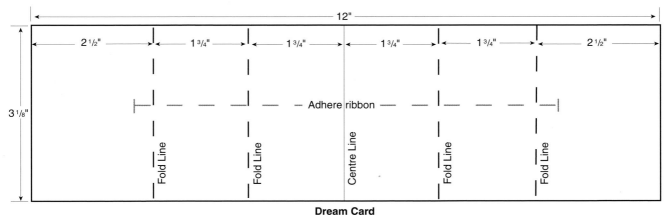

Dream Card
Folding Diagram

Envelope

Stamp text across top edge of envelope flap. Cut scrapbook paper to fit flap below stamped text and punch tip of paper with decorative punch; glue to flap. Fold a 4½-inch length of ribbon in half and secure with double-sided tape; tape to underside of flap. ■

Dream Card
Blank card and envelope, scrapbook paper, stamps, ink pad, decorative punch and ribbon from Anna Griffin Inc.

HOME TWEET HOME

Surprise your feathered friends with an elegant new springtime home.

Design | Susan Stringfellow

Materials

Birdhouse

Coordinating printed card stock: blue floral, white polka dot, brown/blue striped, brown polka dot, solid light blue

4 ivory paper flowers

5⁄8-inch-wide metallic blue ribbon

Coffee stir stick

Light blue watercolour pencil

Black fine-tip marker

Mini round brads: 2 light blue, 2 ivory

Light brown acrylic paint

Sandpaper

1⁄16-inch hole punch

Paintbrush

Foam brush

Adhesive foam squares

Matte medium

Computer and printer (optional)

Instructions

Measure each side of the birdhouse and cut a piece from blue floral card stock to fit; use foam brush and matte medium to adhere card-stock pieces to their corresponding sides of birdhouse. Let dry. Measure base of birdhouse and cut pieces of polka dot card stock for each section. Adhere card-stock strips to base of the birdhouse in the same manner as above. Let dry.

Measure edges of roof. Cut a piece of brown/blue striped card stock to fit each side edge. In the same manner as above, adhere card-stock strips to edges of roof.

Measure length across roof and double that length. In the sample, the measurement is 4 inches, so strips are 8 inches long. Cut six pieces of brown/blue striped card stock 1½ x length measurement. Measure and mark on each strip a line every ¼ inch and then 1 inch, alternating between the two measurements. Accordion-fold on lines to create pleats. *Note: The pleats are meant to be random, so they do not need to be measured perfectly.*

Adhere one pleated strip to bottom edge of roof, allowing it to have a ⅛-inch overhang. Repeat on opposite side of roof. Referring to photo and overlapping rows slightly, adhere remaining pleated strips to roof, forming shingles.

Hand-print, or use a computer to generate, the following sentiments on solid light blue card stock: "Room for Rent!," "Free Birdseed!" and "Great View!" Cut a rectangle around each and adhere to brown polka dot card stock. Trim a narrow border on each.

Home Tweet Home
Flowerpot Base

Home Tweet Home
Flowerpot Rim

Paint birdhouse perch and stir stick with light brown paint; let dry. Adhere layered signs to stir stick, allowing space between each. Tie ribbon into a bow onto stir stick; trim ribbon ends. Insert a brad through a flower; adhere flower to stir stick. Adhere stir stick to bottom left on front of birdhouse; trim off excess at bottom edge of birdhouse.

Use provided patterns to trace and cut a flowerpot base and a flowerpot rim from brown polka dot card stock; sand edges. Adhere rim to base. Tie a bow with a small piece of ribbon; trim ribbon ends. Adhere bow to flowerpot. Use foam squares to adhere flowerpot to lower right side of birdhouse.

Use watercolour pencil and paintbrush to paint edges of two flowers light blue; let dry. Insert brads through remaining flowers; adhere flowers above flowerpot. ■

Home Tweet Home
Printed card stock from My Mind's Eye; matte medium from Golden Artist Colors Inc.

JOYFUL

Deliver a happy greeting with a card designed from bright pastel-coloured papers.

Design | Lisa Johnson

Materials
12 x 12-inch green card stock
Floral double-sided printed paper
Coordinating rub-on transfers
Sticker tab
Die-cut tag
Red ribbon
Scrap paper
Rubber stamps: dot background, "friendship," "if friends were flowers, i'd pick you"
Chalk ink pads: green, orange, red
1¾-inch circle punch
Adhesive foam squares
Paper glue

Instructions
Cut an 11 x 5½-inch piece of green card stock; with long side horizontal, score vertical lines 4, 7 and 10 inches from left end. Accordion-fold on scored lines, making first fold a valley fold. Cut a 4 x 5½-inch piece of green card stock and adhere over short flap on first piece with edge against valley fold. Adhere reverse side of centre segments together, forming a 4 x 5½-inch side-fold card with an inside 3 x 5½-inch centre flap.

Referring to photo, use green ink to stamp dot background along length inside card and on card front;

ink edges green. Punch a 1¾-inch circle from centre top of flap.

Apply rub-on transfers inside card, applying a word transfer so it can be seen through punched circle. Stamp "friendship" on printed paper; cut desired shape around word and ink edges orange. Adhere inside card as shown. Mask the word "flowers" with scrap paper and stamp "if friends were i'd pick you" on back inside panel of card with red ink, positioning sentiment near a flower rub-on transfer. Attach fabric tab to folded edge of flap.

Cut a 2½ x 4¾-inch piece of printed paper; ink edges orange. Apply a word rub-on transfer to upper right edge of paper; adhere to card front. Apply a flower rub-on transfer to lower right corner.

Cut off top of "so happy" tag; ink edges green. Wrap ribbon around tag and knot; trim ribbon ends. Use foam squares to adhere tag to card as shown. ■

Joyful

Printed paper, rub-on transfers, sticker tab, die-cut tag and red ribbon from SEI; rubber stamps from A Muse Artstamps; chalk ink pads from Clearsnap Inc.; Zip Dry Paper Glue from Beacon Adhesives Inc.

BIRTHDAY ACCORDION BOOK

Tuck a little gift card in each pocket of this unique birthday gift book.

Design | Tania Willis

Materials
8½ x 11-inch sheet of card stock for background
Complementary printed papers
Complementary card stocks
Word and alphabet stickers
Alphabet stamps
Ink pads
Complementary chalks
Fine-tip markers
Assorted embellishments: staples, mini brads, washers
Complementary ribbons, fibres and printed twist-ties
Seed beads
Craft wire
Clear file folder tab
⅛-inch hole punch
Adhesive dots
Paper glue

Instructions
Lay 8½ x 11-inch card stock on work surface with longer edges at top and bottom. Evenly fold up bottom so that edge is ½ inch from top; crease (this will form the pockets). To create accordion folds, fold the folded card stock in half from top to bottom, folding it away from you (back sides facing); crease. Open up (leave pocket strip folded up) and fold each side in until it touches the centre crease; crease.

Working from left to right, complete pocket flaps, cutting along creases as needed: first panel, fold down right corner of pocket; second, cut a semicircular notch in the top edge; third, tear top edge at an angle; fourth, fold down pocket edge ¾ inch.

Enhance pockets with staples, stickers, journaling, mini brads and other embellishments as desired. When attaching assorted embellishments, pierce only the front layer of the pocket.

Close pocket strip, applying adhesive only along outermost edges of first and fourth panels. Before closing the fourth pocket completely, insert the file folder tab so that tab is visible when book is closed.

Cut a piece of card stock to fit in each pocket; punch holes along one edge and decorate with ribbons and fibres. Add journaling, stamped sentiments, stickers and other embellishments as desired. Stamp "celebrate" on card stock; trim to fit in file folder tab and insert in tab.

Cover front and back covers of book with printed paper. Decorate cover as desired with stickers, beads strung on craft wire, etc. Tie ribbon around book in a bow to hold it closed. ■

happy day

Close your eyes,
make a wish,
take a deep breath,
blow out your candles...

it's time to
celebrate!
happy
birthday

a moment
in time

Birthday Accordion Book

Printed papers from Chatterbox Inc.; washers
and brads from Making Memories; twist-ties
from Pebbles Inc.; stamps from Hero Arts;
chalk ink pads from Clearsnap Inc.

CHRISTMAS SHADE

Holly leaves and berry-red satin ribbon adorn this pleated-paper candle shade.

Design | Kathleen Paneitz

Materials
12 x 12-inch Christmas printed paper
1-inch-wide red satin ribbon
Red raffia
⅛-inch hole punch
Embossing stylus
Paper glue

Instructions
Cut 12 x 12-inch paper in half forming two 6 x 12-inch pieces. Place ribbon along top edge of one piece of paper, positioning ribbon so ½ inch lays on top of paper and remaining half will wrap around and be adhered on reverse side. Adhere ribbon. Repeat for bottom edge. Adhere ribbon to remaining piece of paper in the same manner.

Lay paper printed side facedown; use a ruler and stylus to score a line down height of paper every ½ inch. Repeat for remaining piece. Accordion-fold scored lines on both pieces and connect both sheets of paper together forming a circle.

Punch a ⅛-inch hole in each fold along one edge. *Note: Punch holes just underneath ribbon.* Thread raffia through holes and pull gently to gather top forming a lampshade. Tie raffia in a bow. ■

Christmas Shade
Printed paper from Anna Griffin Inc.; raffia from ANW Crestwood/Paper Adventures.

LEARN TO RIP PAPER

Given all the great cutting products on the market, why would anyone want to just tear their paper? Discover why for yourself with this fun and creative technique.

By | Leslie Frederick

Torn paper adds texture and dimension to cards, scrapbook pages and other paper art forms. It gives us an opportunity to touch the material we are working with as well as giving our project a unique look. Most importantly, it's fun! Tearing is not an exact science by any means, but learning a few easy techniques can help even a beginner tear like a pro.

Card with torn paper (above) and the same card with cut paper (below).

The Grain

Before getting to the actual process of tearing, it is helpful to envision how paper is made. Making handmade paper entails soaking fibres that are then mixed with water and other additives in a vat to create a pulp. The pulp is dipped out of the vat using a screen in a wooden frame. The screen allows the liquid to drain. Excess liquid is removed by pressing the fibres with absorbent sheets. The new page of paper is pressed between boards and then hung to dry. Many beautiful papers are imported from Thailand, India and Japan, where papermaking has been elevated to an art form.

Modern paper mills add bleach for white paper or dyes for the vast array of colours, and then use large metal cylinders to press out the moisture and create a uniform thickness. The grain on manufactured paper is easier to determine because of this process.

It is important to understand that paper has a grain. Just like fabric in which the threads run horizontally and vertically, so do the fibres in paper. To determine the direction of the paper grain, place the paper on a flat surface and roll it until one side meets the other. Release the sheet and roll it from bottom to top. The roll with the least resistance constitutes the direction of the grain. Tearing with the grain will almost always be easier than tearing against the grain. For a consistent look in a project, you should always tear in the same direction, either against the grain or with the grain. After a few tears, you'll be able to determine whether you're tearing with or against the grain by the look of the torn edge. Handmade paper does not usually have a well-defined grain. For this reason, it is best to add moisture to the paper before tearing it. This makes it easier for the fibres to separate from one another. The beauty of torn handmade paper is those pesky fibres, which provide a soft edge to the project.

Paper torn with the grain (above) and paper torn against the grain (below)

Accenting the edge

Lightweight card stock torn in squares or rectangles to use as photo mats or card accents is the easiest project for beginners. Tearing a strip of paper for the bottom of a scrapbook page can create the look of sand at the beach, grass at the park or snow from your favourite sledding hill.

To tear paper, hold down one side with your nondominant hand and tear toward you with your dominant hand. The weight of your hand pressing down on the paper provides the tension necessary to help you tear in a relatively straight line. If you prefer a more defined torn edge, drawing a light pencil line will weaken the fibres along the line, making it easier to tear the paper.

Tips & Techniques

- When tearing around a curve or when tearing delicate papers such as vellum, use the ball of your thumb on your nondominant hand to prevent the tear from progressing too far. Walk your thumb around the inside edge as you tear and go slowly.

- If the paper you are tearing has a white core or white backing, experiment with tearing in different directions to prevent the white edge from appearing on the right side of your work.

- Tear out squares from scraps and use them along with leftover sticker letters to create a whimsical look for cards or scrapbook projects. Another use for torn shapes is the popular collage look, used in all manner of paper projects these days.

- Save scraps of paper from projects to practice tearing techniques. Like any other skill, the more paper you tear, the better control you'll have over your edges.

Another type of product that gives a unique torn look is paper that has a **kraft-paper base**. As you tear this paper, it reveals a brown edge, as opposed to white. This is an authentic look for heritage and outdoor projects. A variety of specialty papers is widely available, and each one will create a unique look when torn.

Vellum is another favourite type of paper to tear. Soft torn shapes from white vellum, layered over blue paper, is one of the best ways to create the look of clouds. When tearing vellum, make sure to keep the ball of your thumb from the hand that is not tearing close to the edge of your piece, walking the thumb around your project. Vellum tears quickly, making it easier for a tear to get away from you.

Two-tone card stock often has a white core. When you tear paper of this type, you may end up with a white edge. If the white edge is not part of the look you want, you can cover it by using a chalking tool or cotton swab to apply chalk. Rubber-stamp ink brushed on the edge of the paper directly from the ink pad or with a brush is another way to soften a white edge. Sometimes heavyweight card stock with a glimmer or glitter surface has an inner core of a totally different colour—for example, a copper metallic paper with a blue core that could make incredible fall accents when torn.

Flannel paper creates wonderful torn accents, but you will need to tear from the wrong (paper backing) side. Drawing your shape lightly with a pencil is important when working with flannel paper because the nap on the right side prevents you from seeing the tearing pattern.

Apply chalk to torn edge with applicator.

Apply ink directly to torn edge using dauber or small ink pad.

Mulberry paper is another great paper for tearing. The soft fibres pulled from this beautiful paper are what entice many paper crafters to try tearing it. The trick to tearing mulberry paper is the addition of a small amount of water to your paper. Score the edge you want to tear by lightly folding along the tear line and pressing the fold with your thumb and index finger. Moisten a cotton swab or fine liner paintbrush with just a bit of water and "paint" along the scored line. Rather than pulling the paper toward you as in a conventional tear, gently separate the paper along the V-fold of the scored line. This pulling apart is what separates the fibres for that soft, lovely look. Torn mulberry paper is a popular embellishment for wedding invitations, bridal and birth announcements and anniversary cards, as well as for mats for heritage photos.

Some people are hesitant to try tearing for fear that they won't do it correctly, but this is the beauty of torn paper—there is no right or wrong when tearing, and it is the variety that gives torn paper its unique appearance. As you begin to tear elements for your paper crafting, you'll find that it becomes addictive. ■

To tear mulberry paper: lightly score paper, apply water with brush, gently separate paper along wet fold.

Tearing Tools

Ruler: a ruler is a great help when the torn line needs to be straight. For a perfect torn deckle edge, try The Tearing Edge ruler by Stampin' Up! A multitude of combinations is available using this tool to create different looks for your torn-paper projects.

To use a ruler for tearing, hold the paper and the ruler down and tear the paper toward you, pressing against the ruler. You may find that standing helps you distribute your weight more easily along the ruler's surface to create a more even torn edge.

Depending on how you layer your torn edges, you can get a variety of looks from one ruler.

Water brushes: tearing mulberry paper requires the use of an applicator. Many companies manufacture water brushes, which look like standard paintbrushes with a clear tube barrel. To fill a water brush, unscrew the barrel from the brush, squeeze the barrel and submerse it in a container of water. Water is sucked into the barrel when released. After the barrel is full and the brush cap is replaced, a light squeeze will release the water to the brush tip, allowing control of the amount of liquid that flows onto the paper.

Chalk: chalk is a useful addition to your torn-paper toolbox. When working with a white edge, you have the option of shading it with chalk. Craf-T Products has acid-free Decorating Chalks in a myriad of colours, perfect for paper projects. The Stencil Collection also sells Studio Basics Pastels with a built-in fixative so you won't need to seal your finished work.

If you aren't crazy about chalk all over your hands, visit www.pebblesinc.com and order their 3-Prong Applicator. Three wire prongs grip a small cotton pompom, keeping your fingers clean and providing more control over where your chalk is placed than you'll have when using a cotton swab.

Ink Applicators: if you prefer an inked edge for your torn paper, consider investing in dual-tipped ink applicators. Tsukineko's Dauber Duos are acid-free pigment ink with long-lasting colour that will hold up on any project. The two-colour tips contain complementary colours, allowing you to add subtle colour to the look of your torn edge. Tsukineko also manufactures Sponge Daubers. Simply tap the sponge tip onto your favourite ink pad and apply the ink to the torn edge.

DAD & ME DESK SET

Photos of loved ones are a wonderful addition to this coordinating desk set that includes a trinket jar, double frame and clock.

Design | Sandy Rollinger

Materials

Small clock
Small glass jar
Double-photo frame with paper clip holder
5 x 7-inch brown corrugated card with envelope
10 x 12-inch brown gift bag
Card stock: brown, black
Lime green paper
White tissue paper
Stickers: alphabet tag, masculine-themed images
    and words
Buttons: tan, grey
Fibres: gold, green
Metallic pigment ink pads: gold, copper
Highly opaque black paint
Paintbrush
Craft sponge
Paper crimper
Decoupage medium
Acid-free paper glue
Gem glue

Clock

Tear small pieces of tissue paper; use decoupage medium and paintbrush to adhere pieces to front, back and sides of clock, making sure not to cover clock battery opening. Once dry, paint clock black; let dry.

With craft sponge, apply gold and copper ink over raised areas. Tear two small pieces of lime green paper; adhere near bottom of clock with paper glue.

Attach desired stickers to front of clock; glue buttons to front of clock randomly. Wrap fibres around clock base; tie a knot and trim ends. Glue a large button on top of knot.

Photo Holder

Paint photo holder black; let dry. With craft sponge, apply gold and copper inks randomly to photo holder. Cut ½-inch-wide strips of lime green paper; crimp strips and glue around photo openings.

Tear rectangles from lime green paper to fit into paper clip holders at bottom of holder; adhere with paper glue. Let dry.

Add desired stickers around photo openings. Use gem adhesive to adhere fibres and buttons around photo openings.

Pencil Jar Holder

Paint glass jar black; let dry. With craft sponge, apply gold and copper inks randomly to jar. Tear four small pieces of lime green paper; adhere one piece to each side of jar. Cut four small pieces of black card stock and crimp each piece; glue one piece to each side of jar.

Attach a word sticker to each side; adhere buttons near stickers. Wrap fibres around jar rim; tie a knot and trim ends. Glue a button on top of knot.

Gift Bag

Cut a 6¾ x 8¼-inch rectangle from brown card stock and run it through paper crimper. Use paper glue to adhere rectangle to front of bag. Cut an uneven rectangle from lime green paper slightly smaller than crimped rectangle. Adhere onto crimped rectangle.

Tear a 4¼ x 5-inch rectangle from black card stock; adhere onto lime green paper at a slight angle. Use a craft sponge to apply gold ink over all papers on bag; let dry.

Attach desired stickers onto bag randomly; glue buttons on bag as desired. Attach "DAD" alphabet tag stickers toward centre of bag. Embellish upper left corner of papers with fibres and a button.

Card

Follow same instructions as for bag using smaller rectangles of paper. Wrap fibres through card and tie a knot along fold; glue a button on top of knot. ■

Dad & Me Desk Set
Alphabet tag stickers from EK Success; ink pads and paint from Jacquard Products/Rupert, Gibbon & Spider Inc.; Paper-Tac, Glass, Metal & More and Liquid Laminate from Beacon Adhesives Inc.

CHERISH ACCORDION BOOK

Create instant vintage with walnut ink and twine. Place cherished mementos on the uniquely folded pages.

Design | Deanna Hutchison

Materials
3 (8½ x 11-inch) sheets beige card stock
5½ x 11-inch off-white printed paper
2 (4½ x 4½-inch) squares cardboard
1½ x 3-inch cork
Small envelope
15 inches hemp cord
20 inches jute
Skeleton leaf
Decorative T-pin
Rubber stamps: alphabet, desired sentiment
Brown ink pad
Seed beads: 2 dark amber, 2 light amber
"Cherish" definition image
Typewriter letter sticker
Photo mounts
Craft sponge
Adhesive dots
Craft glue
Glue stick

Instructions
Cut printed paper into two 5½-inch squares; centre a piece of cardboard on reverse side of one square and adhere. Cut corners and fold down printed paper; adhere with craft glue and let dry. Repeat for remaining piece.

Cut the three pieces of beige card stock to 8½ inches square; save scraps. Fold each square in half twice and score lines; unfold. Fold each square in half once diagonally; score lines and unfold. Assemble pages by using a glue stick to adhere upper left corner of one square to lower right corner of another lining up horizontal and vertical scored lines; adhere upper left corner of remaining square to lower right corner of middle square so that all three squares are connected. Fold pages up by following folds; set aside.

Apply brown ink to entire surface of front and back covers. Centre and attach jute to inside back cover with photo mounts. Glue pages on top of back cover with craft glue; glue top cover on and square up corners.

To embellish front cover, tear a piece of cork and adhere to top left corner; trim edges and apply brown ink to surface. Apply brown ink to small envelope and skeleton leaf; attach leaf at an angle. Use an adhesive dot to attach T-pin in upper right corner.

Apply brown ink to hemp cord; wrap cord around envelope three times threading seed beads on randomly. Secure ends of cord in back and attach envelope angled on cover. Tear and ink "Cherish" definition; adhere to top of envelope.

Cut a 3½ x 2½-inch rectangle from beige card stock; tear off bottom edge and apply brown ink to sides. Stamp desired sentiment on rectangle. Cut another 1 x 2-inch piece of beige card stock; fold in half and stamp "PULL" on one side. Apply ink to surface and glue tab onto short side of torn rectangle. If desired, embellish inside pages. Tie book to secure. ∎

Cherish Accordion Book
Printed paper from Pebbles Inc.;
T-pin from EK Success; "Cherish"
definition from Making Memories.

LOVE & KISSES FRAME

Torn paper and sanded edges create a trendy, distressed look on the front of this paper-covered wooden frame.

Design | Heather D. White

Materials
8-inch-square wooden frame
Printed papers, including words
Love paper cutouts
Sandpaper
Double-sided tape

Instructions
Cut printed paper to fit front, back and edges of frame, including edges around photo opening. Lightly sand edges and surfaces of paper. Adhere paper to frame with double-sided tape.

Tear an 8 x 3½-inch strip of a different printed paper and an 8 x 4-inch strip of words printed paper. Trim both strips to fit around photo opening. Lightly sand edges and surfaces of paper. Adhere words printed paper to frame with double-sided tape. Adhere other paper strip over words with double-sided tape.

Arrange cutouts, and cut and torn pieces of printed paper to front of frame. Lightly sand edges and surfaces of cutouts and paper pieces. Adhere cutouts and paper pieces to frame with double-sided tape. ■

love and

XOXO

kisses

Love & Kisses Frame
Printed papers and paper
cutouts from Pebbles Inc.

EASTER DELIGHTS PAINT CANS

Who needs baskets when you can fill these cute cans with Easter treats?

Designs | Mary Ayres

Materials

2 (1-quart) paint cans
Pastel shades of green, blue and yellow card stock
Gingham printed papers: yellow, green
White corrugated paper
Dimensional baby-themed star and heart stickers
Easter sentiment rub-on transfers
Pink and purple bunny die cuts
Purple ink pad
Ribbon: ⅝-inch-wide pink gingham, ⅝-inch-wide purple gingham, 1¼-inch-wide sheer white wire-edge
White cord
2 white pompoms
8 mini round silver brads
2 (⅛-inch) silver round eyelets with eyelet setter
Silver glitter spray
Hole punches: 1/16-inch, ⅛-inch
Pinking shears
Craft knife
Paper glue
Project note: Ink edges of all papers.

Happy Easter Paint Can

Cut corrugated paper to fit around paint can; adhere in place. Use pinking shears to cut a 3 x 3½-inch rectangle from green card stock; cut a ¾-inch vertical slit in each corner of rectangle with craft knife. Spray blue card stock with silver glitter; let dry. Tear a 2½-inch square from sprayed card stock and glue to green piece, making sure not to cover vertical slits. Punch a 1/16-inch hole in each corner of blue piece; insert brads. Attach dimensional star sticker and a heart sticker inside blue square.

Insert purple gingham ribbon through top and bottom slits; wrap ribbons around can and tie bows on left side. Trim ends in V-notches.

Cut a 3-inch circle from yellow gingham paper with pinking shears; glue to top of can. Wrap sheer white ribbon around bottom of can and tie into a bow at top; trim ends in V-notches.

Apply an Easter sentiment rub-on transfer onto pink bunny die cut; punch a ⅛-inch hole in bunny neck and attach an eyelet. Glue pompom to bunny as tail; insert white cord through eyelet and tie into a bow around sheer ribbon at top of can.

Cottontail Paint Can

Follow basic instructions as for "Happy Easter" paint can, but use yellow card stock instead of green, pink gingham ribbon instead of purple gingham, green gingham paper instead of yellow gingham and purple bunny die cut instead of pink bunny. Tie pink gingham ribbon on right side of can instead of left. ■

Easter Delights Paint Cans
Printed papers from Hot Off The Press; stickers from K&Company; bunny die cuts from Die Cuts With A View; rub-on transfers from Royal & Langnickel; glitter spray from Krylon; Zip Dry Paper Glue from Beacon Adhesives Inc.

TODAY'S THE DAY

Dried flower stickers combined with metal rimmed tags make ideal card embellishments.

Design | Janice Musante

Materials

6½ x 5-inch blank card with envelope, purchased
Printed papers: friendship themed, crackle, copper
Alphabet epoxy circle stickers
"TODAY'S THE DAY!" vellum sentiment
Metal-edge vellum tags: 2 (1½-inch) square, 1 (2½ x 1½-inch) rectangle
4 (3-inch) lengths raffia, natural colour
5 natural dried flowers, purchased
Dye ink pads: brown, olive green
Brads: 4 brass round, 1 copper metallic square, 1 gold square
1/16-inch hole punch
Laminating machine
Paper glue

Card

Centre and adhere a 5¾ x 4¼-inch piece of crackle paper to a 6⅛ x 4¾-inch piece of copper paper; adhere to card front. Cut two 1¼-inch squares from copper paper; adhere to square tags. Laminate dried flowers; cut small borders. Adhere one flower to each square tag. Place square tags on card front as shown and punch a 1/16-inch hole through centre top of each, going through all layers except back flap of card; insert brass brads. Tie a 3-inch length of raffia around each brad; trim and fray raffia ends.

Cut a 5¾ x 2-inch piece of friendship-themed paper; tear off top edge and adhere to card 1 inch from bottom edge of copper paper. Cut a 5¾ x ½-inch strip of copper paper; tear off top edge and adhere to bottom edge of friendship-themed paper.

Attach stickers to bottom of card to spell "CELEBRATE." Tear a rectangle around vellum sentiment; ink edges with olive green ink. Use square brads to attach sentiment to card at an angle as shown. Adhere a dried flower to card between square tags. Ink card edges with both inks.

For inside card, tear a desired-size strip of friendship-themed paper; adhere inside card. Trim edges.

Envelope

For envelope, adhere a torn strip of copper paper to bottom of envelope front. Trim edges. Cut a piece of copper paper to fit rectangle tag and adhere to tag. Adhere remaining flowers to tag. Insert brass brads through each end of tag; tie a 3-inch raffia length around each brad. Trim and fray raffia ends. Adhere tag to lower left side of envelope. ■

Today's the Day
Printed papers from Hot Off The Press; epoxy stickers from K&Company; vellum sentiment and metal-edge tags from Making Memories; square brads from Jo-Ann Stores Inc.; Zip Dry Paper Glue from Beacon Adhesives Inc.

REFLECTIONS

Reflect a fun image with trendy stamped mirrors.

Design | Helle Greer

Materials

10 x 10-inch wooden mirror
Card stock
Coordinating printed papers
Assorted rubber stamps
Alphabet rub-on transfers
Assorted colours of ink pads
Decorative rub-on transfers
Word stickers
Metal embellishments
Cancelled postage stamps
Decorative trims
Acrylic paint in desired colour
Paintbrush
Craft knife
Clear dimensional adhesive

Instructions

Paint wooden portions of mirror in desired colour. Apply a second coat if needed. Let each coat dry thoroughly.

Tear several pieces of card stock and various pieces of printed papers. Lay them on wooden mirror in desired layout. Once layout has been determined, use craft knife to trim edges evenly with edges of mirror.

Ink paper edges; adhere papers to mirror. Embellish mirror as desired with rubber stamps, dimensional embellishments, stickers, etc.

Glue decorative trim around mirror. Apply a coat of decoupage medium to seal papers and embellishments. Let dry thoroughly. ■

Reflections

Printed papers from Chatterbox Inc. and 7gypsies; rubber stamps from Inkadinkado, Hampton Art and Las Vegas Stamps; rub-on transfers, metal embellishments and stickers from Making Memories; stickers from Karen Foster Design and Creative Imaginations; dimensional adhesive from JudiKins.

TRICK OR TREAT CARD

Create a fun Halloween greeting card with torn paper and quick machine stitching.

Design | Mary Ayres

Materials
Card stock: black, yellow, orange, white
Vellum
White envelope
Black fine-tip marker
Sewing machine with black thread
Masking tape
Permanent fabric glue
Computer and printer (optional)

Instructions
Form a 5 x 7-inch side-fold card from black card stock. Tear 4½ x 2-inch rectangles from white and yellow card stock. Hand-print, or use a computer to generate, "trick or treat" on orange card stock; tear a 4½ x 3-inch rectangle centred around words. Glue white piece across top of card and yellow piece across bottom; glue orange piece across centre.

Cut a 4¼ x 6¼-inch piece of vellum and, using pattern, cut candy corn shape from centre. Place vellum on card and secure in place with masking tape. Machine stitch around inside and outside edges of vellum; remove tape.

Hand-print, or use a computer to generate, "trick or treat" on orange card stock; tear a 1½-inch-wide rectangle around words. Tear same size piece from yellow card stock and glue to back of orange piece. Attach both pieces to left side of envelope. ■

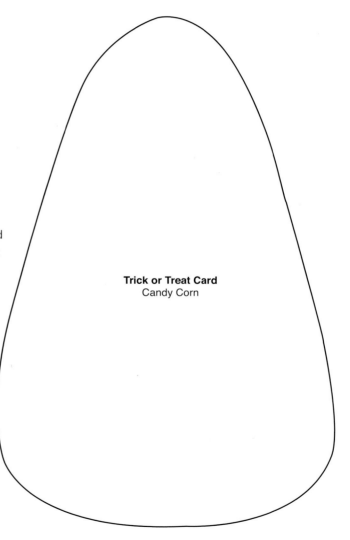

Trick or Treat Card
Candy Corn

Trick or Treat Card
Fabri-Tac Glue from Beacon Adhesives Inc.

LEARN TO DISTRESS PAPER

When you just can't find that one perfect paper design for your project, try altering the original look of the paper by distressing it.

By | Connie Petertonjes

There are many different techniques for distressing paper. Experimenting with these methods allows you to match the look of paper with whatever theme and feel you are trying to create.

Scratch It

Scratching paper can transform even a whimsical pattern into one that is perfect for a project with a vintage theme. Several methods are used to scratch paper. For the most drastic look, take the point of the scissors blade or a needle and literally just scratch the paper, being careful not to tear holes. If this look is too distressed, try scratching paper with a wire brush or steel wool. The result is less dramatic depending on how hard you rub the steel over your paper. The most subtle way to scratch paper is by using sandpaper. You can sand the edges of the paper or the entire piece to remove some of the colour.

Scrapper's Block
from PM designs

Varying the grit of the sandpaper will allow you to achieve several different looks.

Ink It

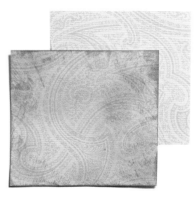

Inking is a great way to alter paper. Use a regular dye ink pad and a cotton ball to apply ink to the edges of your paper. You can also dab ink over the entire sheet using a cotton ball or a stipple brush. If you are slightly more adventurous, try using inks specifically designed for distressing paper. These do not dry as fast as regular dye inks, so you have more time to feather the ink and give it a softer edge. Different colours of ink will result in different finished looks. Black and grey inks will give your paper a grungy look while browns and tans will age your paper.

Distress ink pads and distress powders from Ranger Industries Inc.

Soak It

For a more vintage feel, soak your paper in strong tea or coffee. You will achieve different looks depending on how long you let it soak. For darker tints, skip the coffee and tea and use walnut ink to age your paper. You can vary  the darkness of the walnut ink depending on how much water you add to the walnut ink and also on the length of time you soak your paper. Be aware that walnut ink will stain an unprotected work surface as well as your fingers. Wearing gloves while working with walnut ink is advised.

Paint It

Using paints to distress paper will give your paper a shabby-chic look. The key to using paints to distress is using a small amount of paint. You will get the best results by lightly brushing the paint on the paper using an almost dry brush. Try foam and bristle brushes for different looks. You can always add more paint if you have not achieved the desired effect; however, it is not possible to take the paint off the paper if you use too much paint from the start.

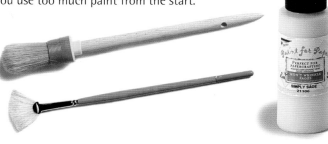

Distressing kit from Making Memories

Tear & Crumple It

Tearing and crumpling are both easy to do and do not require special tools. Tearing paper with a white core will give your paper an interesting border which can be left as is, inked for added colour or curled by running your fingernail along the edge or by using an edge distresser. Crumpling adds texture to a paper which would otherwise look flat. Wad the paper into a ball. Carefully open the wad and smooth the paper using your hands or the flat edge of a ruler. Be cautious when un-wadding your paper. A lightweight paper may tear around the edges. The tears do not necessarily look bad, though. They can actually give the paper more character and contribute to the distressed result.

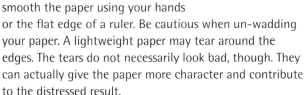

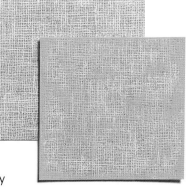

Large Snowflake
Clipboard, page 70

Fake It

Short on time? There are many companies that offer papers that are already distressed. You can find just about any type paper you need with faux sanded edges, scratched surfaces and hand-dyed looks. Very few people will be able to tell that you used the paper "as is." You will achieve a similar distressed look in a lot less time with little effort.

Next time you are browsing through your paper stacks, unable to find the perfect paper, try these distressing techniques. Try combining them for a fabulous, one-of-a-kind look. For example, crumple your paper and then sand the flattened piece, or sand your paper then ink it. You will not only end up with a look that is unique to your project, but you might also find a use for some of your older, overlooked papers. Distressing techniques add a lot of interest to your creations and most can be done without much extra effort. ∎

GIFT ORGANIZER

A thrift-store find inspires the design of the handy organizer.

Design | Cathy Schellenberg

Materials

Wooden box
Card stock: dark turquoise, light turquoise, turquoise, light blue, brown
Printed papers
Blank notebook paper
Chipboard letters to spell "gift"
Flower button
Card-stock tab
Black fine-tip marker
Ribbons: brown sheer, blue textured, brown woven
Alphabet rub-on transfers
Brown dye ink pad
Scallop-edge scissors
Corner rounder
Screwdriver to fit hardware on box
Foam brush
Sewing machine with black thread
Decoupage medium
Adhesive dimensional dot
Computer and printer (optional)

Instructions

Remove hardware from box; set aside. Cut pieces of printed papers to fit box sides and lid; use foam brush and decoupage medium to adhere papers to corresponding sections. Let dry. Reattach hardware.

Cut a 5⅝ x 3½-inch piece of turquoise card stock; round left-side corners and ink edges. Adhere to front of box, aligning right edges. Cut a 4½ x 2-inch piece of light turquoise card stock; round left-side corners and ink edges; adhere to box front, aligning right edges.

Cut a 5½ x 3½-inch piece of brown card stock, trimming top, bottom and left edges with scallop-edge scissors. Adhere to box front, aligning right edges. Cut a 1-inch-wide strip of printed paper long enough to fit across front of box; ink edges and adhere centred to box front.

Apply alphabet rub-on transfers to spell "organizer" on lower right corner of box. Wrap sheer ribbon around box

and knot on left side. Tie short lengths of remaining ribbons next to sheer ribbon knot; trim ribbon ends at an angle.

Place chipboard letters faceup on light turquoise paper; trace around. Cut out paper letters and adhere to front of chipboard letters. Ink edges and adhere to front of box. Thread a small piece of brown woven ribbon through flower button; trim ribbon ends and use the dimensional dot to adhere button above the letter "i."

Cut several 5½ x 4½-inch rectangles from turquoise and dark turquoise card stock. Use card-stock tab as a template to cut a tab from light blue card stock for each rectangle; adhere card-stock tabs to rectangles.

Decorate rectangles with cut strips of printed papers and card stock. Embellish rectangles with machine-stitching.

Hand-print, or use a computer to generate, an information card on blank notebook paper for each person's birthday including their name, birth date, anniversary and special interests. Cut a rectangle around each. Ink edges and adhere one to each rectangle. Insert rectangles inside box. ■

Gift Organizer

Printed papers and flower button from Prima Marketing Inc.; chipboard letters from Delish Designs; rub-on transfers from 7gypsies; card-stock tab from SEI.

BEST FRIENDS CARD & TAG

A flower-embellished card is distressed and aged with love. What a perfect way to send a favourite friend your thoughts.

Design | Heidi Larsen

Materials

Card stock: cream, pale pink
Double-sided dark red/light blue polka dot printed card stock
Coordinating "friends" rectangle
Black "forever" rub-on transfer
"Best Friends" fabric label
Brown dye ink pad
¼-inch-wide dark red gingham ribbon
Gunmetal round brads: 4 mini, 2 large
Punches: 1-inch circle, large daisy, ¹⁄₁₆-inch hole, ⅛-inch hole
Glue stick

Card

Form a 4¼ x 5½-inch side-fold card from cream card stock; ink edges. Cut a 2⅝ x 3⅜-inch rectangle from double-sided card stock; ink edges on light blue side and adhere near centre of card front. Adhere "friends" rectangle to upper right corner; punch a ¹⁄₁₆-inch hole through each corner. Insert mini brads.

Punch two large daisies from double-sided card stock; ink edges on dark red side. Use a pencil to gently roll daisy petals upward.

Layer daisies on top of each other and referring to photo for placement, adhere to card front, applying adhesive to centres only. Punch a 1-inch circle from pale pink card stock; ink edges. Adhere to flower centre. Punch a ⅛-inch hole through flower centre and insert large brad.

Apply "forever" rub-on transfer to lower right corner of card front. Punch two ⅛-inch holes approximately ½ inch apart along right edge of light blue printed card stock; thread a piece of ribbon through each hole and tie knots. Trim ribbon ends.

Tag

Cut a 2¾ x 5¼-inch piece of cream card stock; cut off top corners diagonally, forming a tag. Ink edges. Cut two 2¾ x ½-inch strips from double-sided card stock; ink edges on dark red side. Adhere one strip ⅛ inch above bottom edge of tag; adhere remaining strip 1¾ inches above first strip.

Punch two large daisies from double-sided card stock; ink edges on light blue polka dot side. In the same manner as for card, gently roll petals upward. Layer daisies on top of each other and adhere to bottom of tag. Punch a 1-inch circle from double-sided card stock; ink edges on dark red side and adhere to flower centre. Punch a ⅛-inch hole through flower centre; insert large brad. Ink edges of "Best Friends" fabric label; attach to tag above daisy.

Cut a ⅞ x 1⅝-inch rectangle from pale pink card stock; ink edges. Cut a 1¼ x 2-inch rectangle from double-sided card stock; ink edges on light blue side. Layer and adhere rectangles together. Adhere rectangles to centre top of tag, letting ends extend past top of tag. Punch two ⅛-inch holes through bottom of pale pink rectangle; thread ribbon through holes and tie a knot. Trim ribbon ends. ■

Best Friends Card & Tag

Printed card stock, "friends" rectangle and fabric label from My Mind's Eye Inc.

SUMMERTIME THANKS

Crumpled paper mimics the look of a sand dune at the shore.

Design | Susan Stringfellow

Materials
Card stock: light blue, cream
Lighthouse transparency
Small cork rectangle
Alphabet rubber stamps
Ink pads: black, brown
Small decorative metal bar
Twill tape
Blue and metallic fibres
Light blue mini brads
Beige sand-textured paint
Paintbrush
⅛-inch hole punch
Double-sided tape
Clear dimensional adhesive

Instructions
Form a 6 x 6-inch side-fold card from light blue card stock; ink edges brown. Using a dry brush, lightly brush sand-textured paint across lower half of card; let dry.

For added sand texture, tear two pieces of cream card stock to fit horizontally across card. Dampen each strip with water and crumple up; let dry. Smooth each piece out and paint both with two coats of sand-textured paint.

Let dry. Attach one piece across bottom of card and trim edges evenly; tear the other piece so it is slightly smaller than larger piece and adhere it to top of first piece.

Lay lighthouse transparency on upper left portion of card, allowing top edge of small sand-textured strip to overlap transparency. Do not adhere transparency yet.

Cut three 2½-inch lengths of twill tape; wrap one length around centre of decorative metal bar and, referring to photo, punch a ⅛-inch hole and insert a mini brad to secure. Repeat with remaining lengths of twill tape, securing them above and below centre piece. Cut two 5½-inch lengths of fibres and tie them between twill pieces.

Use black ink to stamp one of the following words on each piece of twill tape: "sun," "surf" and "sea." Adhere metal bar along right side of transparency, so adhesive will also secure transparency. Secure twill pieces with double-sided tape.

Use black ink to stamp "sand" onto cork rectangle; rub brown ink on edges and adhere rectangle to lower right corner of card on top of sand-textured card stock. Use brown ink to stamp "thank you" along right side of card. ∎

Summertime Thanks

Paint from DecoArt Inc.;
transparency from Altered Pages;
metal bar from K&Company.

MINI BAG

This is a cute way to give a small gift to a little girl or a friend. It also makes for a great shower favour.

Design | Kim Hughes

Materials
Small kraft paper bag with handles
Printed papers: red, striped, flowers
4 silk flowers
4 white buttons
Jute
Scallop-edge scissors
Corner rounder
Small hole punch
Sanding block
Paper glue

Instructions
Cut a piece of striped paper to fit front of bag. Lightly sand edges and glue in place. Cut a ¾-inch-wide piece of red printed paper for border on front of bag. Lightly sand edges and glue horizontally to front of bag.

Cut a 1½ x 2-inch piece of flower printed paper; round top two corners and cut a scalloped edge across bottom. Lightly sand edges. Tie a single knot with jute through each white button. Glue buttons to flowers and glue three flowers to lower right front of bag.

Punch a small hole at top of tag and add a larger loop of jute. Glue fourth flower to top of tag, covering hole. Tie tag to bag. ■

Mini Bag
Printed papers from
Making Memories; flowers
from Prima Marketing Inc.

ROAD SONGS

Prepare for your summer adventures by making a special holder for your personal playlist.

Design | Lisa Johnson

Materials
5½ x 5½-inch note card
Blank CD
Card stock: lime green, cream
Chipboard shapes: road sign, car, numbers
Ribbons
Vintage type alphabet stamps
Ink pads: brown dye, dark brown chalk, brown chalk
Sticky notes
2 large snaps with snap setter
Craft sponge
Corner rounder
¼-inch hole punch
Paper glue
Fabric glue

Instructions
Project note: Ink all edges of this project with brown chalk ink.

Fold card inside out. On front, score 2 inches in from right edge and fold back to create flap. Round all corners on note card.

Trim lime green card stock to 3¾ x 5½ inches and adhere to front of card under flap. Trim ribbons to 5½ inches and adhere across flap with fabric glue, sealing ends as well. Ink ends with brown dye ink.

Trace around road sign chipboard piece onto lime green card stock; cut out. Use sticky notes to mask off a horizontal line as seen in photo. Sponge in line with dark brown ink.

Using vintage alphabet stamps and brown dye ink, stamp letters to spell "route" and "road songs" on cream card stock. Punch out letters to spell "route" and adhere to the road sign. Repeat with "road songs" and adhere in two lines to the ribbon.

Use snap setter to attach snaps to tires of chipboard car and adhere car to lower right corner of front of card. Adhere numbers to road sign and adhere finished sign to front of card over ribbons using a heavy amount of paper glue. Adhere edges of note card together with a thin line of paper glue.

Purchase and download songs as desired onto CD and place CD in case. ■

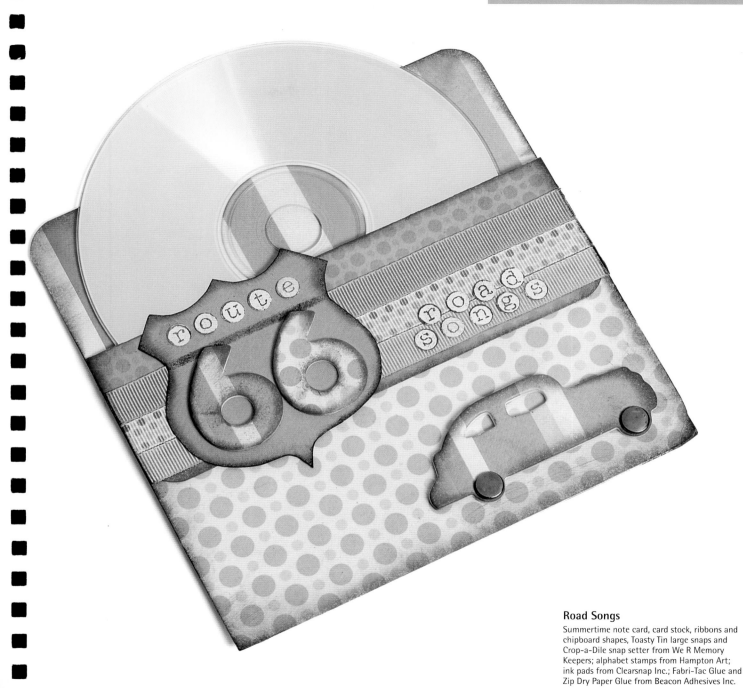

Road Songs

Summertime note card, card stock, ribbons and chipboard shapes, Toasty Tin large snaps and Crop-a-Dile snap setter from We R Memory Keepers; alphabet stamps from Hampton Art; ink pads from Clearsnap Inc.; Fabri-Tac Glue and Zip Dry Paper Glue from Beacon Adhesives Inc.

MERRY CHRISTMAS

Bold colourful prints surround your holiday message of cheer.

Design | Tami Mayberry

Materials

Red card stock
Printed papers: red paisley, green paisley, red stars
Cream self-adhesive mesh
Self-adhesive "Merry Christmas" fabric tag
Laminate chip
¼-inch-wide red gingham ribbon
Gold decorative stud
Mini round brads: 2 red, 2 green
Sandpaper
Corner rounder
¹⁄₁₆-inch hole punch
Adhesive foam tape
Paper glue

Instructions

Form a 4 x 6-inch side-fold card from red card stock. Cut a piece of green paisley paper slightly smaller than card front; round corners and adhere to card front.

Cut a 2 x 5¾-inch piece of red stars paper; sand edges and adhere to left side of card front. Centre and attach a 1⅛ x 5¾-inch strip of mesh on top of red stars paper.

Cut a 2⅞ x 3¾-inch piece of red paisley paper; sand edges and adhere to red card stock. Trim a small border. Punch ¹⁄₁₆-inch holes through corners; insert brads, alternating colours. Adhere a 2⅞-inch length of ribbon across red paisley paper ¾ inch above bottom edge. Adhere to card as shown.

Apply self-adhesive fabric tag to laminate chip; loop ribbon through existing hole. Adhere to card as shown with foam tape. Attach decorative stud to lower right area of card front. ■

Merry Christmas

Printed papers from Flair Designs; self-adhesive mesh from Magic Mesh; brads and ribbon from Creative Impressions; fabric tag from American Traditional Designs; Zip Dry Paper Glue from Beacon Adhesives Inc.

LARGE SNOWFLAKE CLIPBOARD

This functional and decorative project will provide your whole family with a fun way to count down the days to Christmas.

Design | Julia Stainton

Materials

Clipboard
Light green card stock
Printed papers: snowflakes, red/green
Small formal snap stamps
Black ink pad
Manila envelope
Large chipboard snowflake
Black striped ribbon
Rub-on transfers: brown holiday sentiments and decorations, black numbers
Clear acetate snowflakes
Snowflake metal tag
White acrylic paint
Sandpaper
Tab punch
Paintbrush
Sewing machine with white thread
Paper glue

Instructions

Cut snowflakes paper to fit front of clipboard and adhere in place. Trim and sand edges.

Paint edges of clipboard and front clip with white paint; let dry. Paint reverse side of clear snowflakes and front of chipboard snowflake; let dry. Apply brown snowflake rub-on transfers to each point of chipboard snowflake.

Tear away approximately 2 inches from bottom of manila envelope. Machine-stitch bottom closed.

Apply "Have You Been Good?" rub-on transfer to scrap from manila envelope and stitch around edges. Adhere to red/green paper and trim a border; adhere to lower right corner of envelope.

Tie ribbon around chipboard snowflake, attaching metal tag. Cut strip of ribbon to run horizontally across top of clipboard and adhere in place. Adhere scrap of ribbon to lower right of envelope.

Apply rub-on transfers to clipboard and painted clip as desired. Stamp "DAYS LEFT" on top right of envelope. Clip envelope to clipboard.

Adhere chipboard and clear snowflakes to front of clipboard. Using light green card stock and red/green paper, create 12 inserts for envelope. Personalize each insert by writing a special surprise or activity for that day.

Punch 12 tabs from snowflakes paper. Adhere number rub-on transfer to tab and adhere tab to top right on insert. Change insert every day. ∎

Large Snowflake Clipboard

Printed papers and rub-on transfers from Cosmo Cricket; snap stamps from Karen Foster Design; chipboard elements from BasicGrey; acetate snowflake from Heidi Swapp/Advantus Corp.

Learn to Choose Ink for Paper

There are many types of inks available to paper crafters. Which ink to use: pigment, dye, chalk, hybrid or specialty ink? Let's get you started on the way to a well-inked project!

By | Lisa Johnson

Which Ink to Choose?

Sensational effects can be achieved when the correct inks are used in your projects, but where to start? Here are a few questions to help you determine what type of ink to use.

1. Do you need the ink to be acid free and archival quality?

2. Does the project need a fast-drying ink?

3. Does it need to be fade resistant or permanent?

4. How will the ink be applied (stamps, direct to paper (DTP), sponges, watercoloured, etc.)?

5. What is the medium that you will be applying ink to (paper, wood, metal, plastic, etc.)?

With these and other questions, research each company's specifications for their ink to make sure any critical needs are met. Here is some information to help get you started.

Pigment Ink

Most pigment inks are slow to dry, which allows time for you to sprinkle clear embossing powder over any colour to achieve a coordinating embossed image. They are archival, permanent and fade-resistant when heat set. Pigment inks dry on the surface of your medium which gives you more

Pigment ink stamped image and ink pad.

working time on paper to perform various techniques. They are often the scrapbooker's choice when stamping due to their archival qualities.

Dye Ink

These incredible inks are a card creator's favourite due to the fast dry time, ease of use and flexibility in many different applications. Dye inks saturate the medium in which they are applied. If working on a glossy surface paper, using a heat tool will shorten the drying time. Sponging and DTP are most easily accomplished with dye ink. An added bonus of dye ink is the ability to use it for watercolouring. However, for the die-hard archivalist, make sure that you check the manufacturer's specifications to ensure that the product meets your particular needs. Many dye inks, though easier to use, are not fade-resistant and are not permanent; however, most are acid-free. Marvy Uchida and Stampin' Up! offer a large variety of colours on raised felt pads that stack and store easily.

Chalk ink stamped image and ink pads.

Dye ink stamped image and ink pads.

Chalk Ink

This fun ink gives a soft flat chalky appearance that is permanent when heat set. These inks are spectacular when used for a basic chalk resist technique, simple stamping and DTP. This ink is highly recommended for card making and other paper-crafting needs. Chalk ink can be pigment-based or water-based depending on the manufacturer. Pigment-based chalk inks take longer to dry, yet are acid-free. Colorbox's Fluid Chalk ink by Clearsnap, though not archival, is fast drying and comes in a large variety of colours as well as pad sizes, making the ease of use and smooth finish stand out.

Specialty Ink

Watermark, embossing, solvent and hybrid inks are just a few of the specialty inks that allow crafters to achieve many techniques in a simple way. Some of these inks are multifunctional in their use. VersaMark watermark ink by Tsukineko is one of these multitasking inks. Use it to create a watermark image on quality dyed paper, to apply powder mediums, to create an image that will resist ink that is brayered over with dye ink or as a base ink for heat-embossing powder. Top Boss embossing ink by

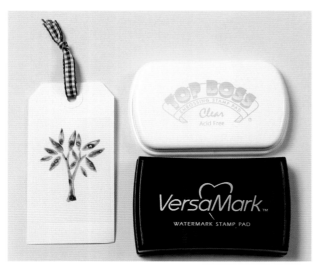

Specialty ink stamped image and ink pads.

Solvent ink pads.

Clearsnap has additional uses besides being an embossing base. It fades after a short time, making it possible to stamp an image and stitch over it or journal around a shape leaving no apparent pattern!

If your needs are to stamp or create an ink image on a nonporous surface then StazOn solvent ink by Tsukineko is the product for you. This ink will set on glass, plastic, metal, stone—pretty much anything you can imagine. Solvent ink is also optimal for use as a base ink for watercolouring. It will not bleed or fade when colours are watercoloured over it, giving the image a crisper appearance.

Experiment with these different inks and the many different mediums that are available. Take time to play and try new things. Personal choice is the final determining factor of what ink to use!

Note: When caring for your inks and ink pads there are many products to choose from. Dye ink usually cleans off with ease; however, some of the other inks can be difficult to remove, from rubber stamps in particular. Always use a product that removes all types of ink and restores rubber stamps to their original appearance. Use with a specially designed scrubber to ensure the desired result. Never use hot water as it may damage the glue holding the rubber surface of the stamp on to the wood block. ∎

Keep your rubber stamps clean.

MULTIPLICITY IN MINUTES

Start with shadow stamps and add another layer or two of contrasting colours to create unique paper for crafting.

Design | Julie Ebersole

Materials

4¼ x 5½-inch white card
Card stock: white, pale yellow, red
Rubber stamps: solid circle, solid square, leaf, flower, flower outline, splatter, various sentiments
Ink pads: pale yellow, pale pink, pale green, yellow, green, red, black, opaque white
Fine iridescent glitter
Red fibres
¼-inch-wide red gingham ribbon
Green and yellow craft thread
Metal-edge flower vellum tag
Eyelets with eyelet setter: ⅛-inch silver, ¼-inch red
Circle punches: ¼-inch, 1¼-inch
Unused pencil eraser
Round craft sponge
Decorative corner punch
Glue pen

Instructions

This "double-time" technique involves randomly stamping geometric and focal images in an all-over pattern on a single sheet of light-colour card stock. The stamped sheet is then cut apart to create multiple projects. When time and quantity are of the essence, this variation of collage can help you produce a number of beautifully coordinated projects in a matter of minutes.

To create the double-time pattern on all pieces in this set, first randomly stamp the solid circle and solid square images onto white card stock using pale colour ink pads. Continue by stamping the leaf and flower images randomly on top of circles and squares using slightly darker colour ink pads. Finally, stamp flower outline and splatter images on top using the darker colour ink pads.

Bookmark

Cut a 1½ x 4-inch strip from stamped card stock; mount strip onto red card stock. Mount again onto a 2 x 5¼-inch piece of pale yellow card stock; cut top two corners of pale yellow card stock to form a tag shape. Fold top section of tag shape down to form a flap and punch a hole through all layers. Attach a red eyelet through hole; loop and knot fibre and craft threads through eyelet.

Thank You Card

Cut a 1⅞-inch square from stamped card stock; cut a 2¼-inch square from red card stock. Punch one corner of red square with decorative corner punch. Tuck stamped

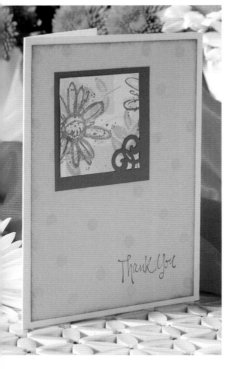

square into decorative corner and adhere to secure.

Trace one of the flower images with glue pen; sprinkle with fine iridescent glitter and let dry. Cut pale yellow card stock 4 x 5¼ inches; use an unused pencil eraser and yellow ink pad to stamp background with polka dots. Apply red ink to edges.

Mount yellow card stock to white card. Stamp sentiment in lower right corner and mount assembled square in upper left corner.

CD Jacket

Cut red card stock to 8½ x 11 inches. Following diagram, cut out CD jacket. Score and fold dashed lines. Lay jacket with outside facing up; stamp entire surface with flower outline image using opaque white ink. Let dry.

Cut a 4-inch square from stamped card stock; apply red ink to edges. Mount square on a 4¼-inch square of pale yellow card stock. Punch a 1¼-inch circle from red card stock; stamp sentiment on circle with opaque white ink. Let dry and glue to metal-edge flower tag. Punch a ⅛-inch hole at top of tag and attach silver eyelet. Punch

a ⅛-inch hole in upper left corner of layered square. Tie metal-edge tag to square using green craft thread.

Assemble CD jacket; wrap a piece of red gingham ribbon around jacket and tie into a bow knotting the ribbon ends. Mount assembled square over ribbon on jacket front. ■

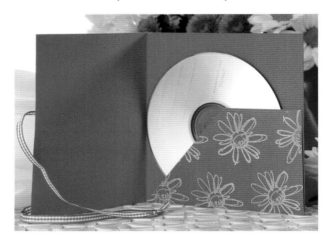

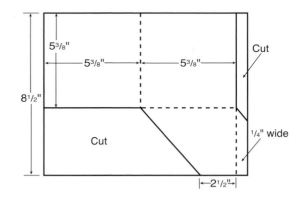

Multiplicity in Minutes
CD Jacket Diagram

a little
something
just
for you

Thank You

Multiplicity in Minutes

Rubber stamps, card stock, ink pads, eyelets, iridescent glitter and red fibre from Stampin' Up!; wrought iron corner punch from EK Success; metal-edge flower tag from Making Memories.

Boo Door Hanger

Grandma will love this Halloween card that doubles as a door hanger. It features a cute ghost created by stamping a child's foot!

Design | Sam Cousins

Materials

Black card stock
Complementary printed papers in Halloween colours
October page torn from small calendar
Black adhesive mesh
Orange "Boo!" ribbon
1-inch white alphabet cutouts or stickers
1-inch round white frame fasteners
Green staples
Clear domed stickers: ⅜-inch, ¾-inch
Fabric "Happy Halloween" label
Craft paints: green, white
White chalk ink pad
Black fine-tip pen
Craft glue

Instructions

Cut printed paper to desired size (sample measures 6¼ x 5½ inches). Tear another piece from a complementary print to overlay the first. Adhere both sheets on black card stock, sandwiching a strip of mesh between printed papers down right edge; tear edges off card stock. Rub torn edges on white chalk ink pad. Secure layers using green staples.

Brush bottom of your child's foot with white paint; have him "stamp" his foot on black card stock. (Heel will be head of ghost; toes will be bottom.) Trim around image; use black fine-tip marker to note name and age along edge, and to draw eye circles and wires for glasses. Adhere ⅜-inch domed stickers over eyes. Tie ribbon in a bow around ghost's neck; adhere ghost to background.

Paint frame fasteners green; when paint is dry, scratch most of it off. Mount frame fasteners over letters to spell "Boo"; top each letter with a ¾-inch domed sticker. Adhere letters to door hanger.

Crumple calendar page; smooth out and adhere in lower right corner. Using green staples, affix fabric Halloween label over calendar page, leaving 31 visible; adhere a ⅜-inch domed sticker over 31. Use green staples to attach ribbon for hanging loop. ∎

Boo Door Hanger
Printed papers from Rusty Pickle; ribbon from
Impress Rubber Stamps; frame fasteners from
Scrapworks; domed stickers, green staples and
paints from Making Memories; alphabet cutouts
from Doodlebug Design Inc.; fabric label from me
& my BIG ideas; chalk ink pad from Clearsnap Inc.

ENCOURAGEMENT KEY CHAINS

Let a friend know how much you care by presenting her with a tiny key chain emblazoned with a kind sentiment.

Designs | Sandra Graham Smith

Materials

2 (1¾ x 2⅝-inch) laminate chips
Tissue paper: light blue, white
Small sheet of aluminum craft metal
Rubber stamps: collage, "Joy," "Gratitude"
Ink pads: pearl green, black
Silver leafing pen
2 silver dragonfly brads
Key punch
2 split rings
Wire cutters
Laminating medium
Craft cement

"Joy"

Stamp white tissue paper with collage stamp using pearl green ink. Spread laminating liquid on laminate chip; lay stamped tissue over top and press tissue into liquid; tear away excess tissue. Apply more laminating liquid on sides and spread a thin layer on top.

Stamp "Joy" sentiment on top of key chain using black ink pad; let dry. Ink edges and draw border around front of key chain using silver leafing pen.

Using key punch, punch largest key from aluminum sheet; cut off top of key and position over hole in key chain; adhere using craft cement. Snip prongs off dragonfly brad using wire cutters; adhere brad in bottom corner of key chain using craft cement. Thread key chain onto split ring.

"Gratitude"

Follow instructions for "Joy" key ring substituting light blue tissue for white and "Gratitude" stamp for "Joy." ■

Encouragement Key Chains

Stamps from Stamper's Anonymous and Hero Arts; leafing pen from Krylon; key punch from The Punch Bunch; laminating medium from Duncan Enterprises.

BUTTERFLY
THANK YOU

*Embossed butterflies float on a glossy
card stock background covered with
an array of colourful pigment ink.*

Design | Brenda Jones

Materials
Card stock: turquoise, white, white glossy
Bright green slide mount
⅞-inch-wide blue/green printed ribbon
Rubber stamps: butterfly, dragonfly, alphabet
Ink pads: watermark, pearlescent tricolour pigment in
    shades of blue/green, blue solvent
Clear embossing powder
Embossing heat tool
Corner rounder
Adhesive dots
Double-sided tape
Adhesive applicator with permanent adhesive cartridges

Instructions
Form a 5 x 6½-inch side-fold card from turquoise card
stock. Cut a 4¾ x 6⅛-inch piece of white card stock;
round corners; adhere to card.

Cut a 3½ x 5¾-inch piece of white glossy card stock;
round corners. Use watermark ink to stamp butterflies
and dragonflies on white glossy rectangle; emboss images
with clear embossing powder. Inking directly to card stock,
drag tricolour ink pad over glossy rectangle, working
diagonally, down and then up until surface is inked as
desired; let dry. Ink edges with blue solvent ink.

Ink edges of slide mount with blue solvent ink; let dry.
Tie ribbon around left side of slide mount; trim ribbon
ends diagonally. Adhere slide mount on top of a butterfly.
Adhere assembled panel to left side of card. Use tricolour
ink to stamp "Thank You" on right side of card. ■

Butterfly Thank You
Rubber stamps from Crafts Etc!/Stampabilities and Plaid Enterprises/All Night Media; ink pads from Tsukineko Inc.; adhesive applicator and adhesive cartridges from Xyron.

A Cool Birthday

This card is simple, easy to make and can be adapted for any season!

Design | Janice Musante

Materials

Dura-Lar plastic film
Black-and-white and turquoise printed papers
Envelope to fit a 4⅞ x 5⅜-inch card
Rub-on transfers: doodles, "Happy," "Birthday!"
Black pearlescent pigment ink pad
Turquoise embossing powder
Black grease pen
Paper flowers: 1 white, 1 turquoise
2 large black-and-white brads
3¾ inches ⅜-inch-wide black-and-white polka dot
    grosgrain ribbon
2 silver faux eyelets
Die-cutting machine and Flower #1A,
    Generic (#13329) die
Embossing heat tool
Double-sided tape
Fabric glue
Paper glue

Instructions

Project notes: *If you smudge the plastic film card or envelope, pour fingernail polish remover over a cotton swab and rub gently. Dry with a soft tissue.*

Form a 4⅞ x 5⅜-inch side-fold card from Dura-Lar.

Use patterns to cut a small flower and a medium flower from turquoise printed papers; ink flower edges. Die-cut four large flowers from black-and-white paper; ink edges. Remove centre flowers from die cuts.

Adhere one large flower to card front; adhere a second large flower to reverse side of card front, covering back of first flower. Repeat to adhere two remaining large flowers to other half of card.

Separate layers of paper flowers. Layer flowers as shown.

Fold ribbon in half; place folded end on back of layered flowers and place all centred on card front. Insert a large brad through centre of all flowers, ribbon end and card front, securing pieces together.

Trim ribbon ends at an angle; apply a small amount of fabric glue to ribbon ends to keep from fraying.

Apply doodles rub-on transfers onto card as shown, making sure no doodles overlap when card is closed. Apply "Happy" rub-on transfer centred inside large flower inside card. Cut a 2⅜ x ⅞-inch piece of Dura-Lar; ink edges and apply "Birthday" rub-on transfer. Adhere "Birthday" tag inside card; adhere silver eyelets to ends of tag.

Take apart premade envelope and use as a template to trace an envelope onto Dura-Lar using a black grease pen. Cut out envelope and assemble using paper glue to adhere flaps.

A Cool Birthday

Dura-Lar from Grafix Plastics; printed papers from me & my BIG ideas, Sandylion Sticker Designs and KI Memories; doodles rub-on transfers, large brads and paper flowers from Making Memories; words rub-on transfers from The C-Thru Ruler Co./Déjà Views; faux eyelets from Jo-Ann Stores Inc.; Brilliance pearlescent ink pad from Tsukineko Inc.; die-cutting machine and die from Ellison.

Attach a strip of double-sided tape along side of envelope front; continue wrapping tape around to back and attach tape alongside on back of envelope. Repeat on opposite side of envelope.

Sprinkle embossing powder on tape; brush off excess and heat with embossing tool to set powder. Layer a small turquoise flower over a small white flower and attach to upper left corner of envelope front with a large brad. ■

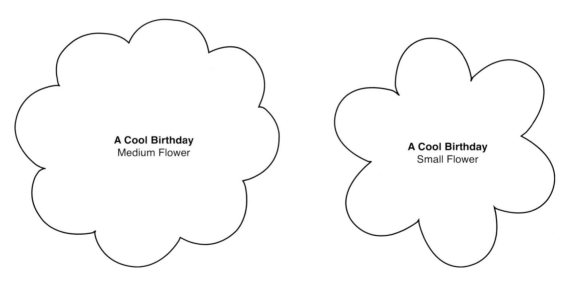

A Cool Birthday
Medium Flower

A Cool Birthday
Small Flower

LEARN TO EMBOSS

Wet and dry embossing are two techniques which often intimidate the average paper crafter. With a little knowledge about the correct tools required for the desired look, embossing can be a versatile technique any level of crafter can learn and use with ease.

By | Connie Petertonjes

Wet or Heat Embossing

Wet or heat embossing is the most common type of embossing. It can also be the more intimidating of the two styles. The many different types of powders and inks can be a turn-off for beginners. There are really only a few key things to remember. First, you need an embossing or a pigment ink instead of a dye ink. Embossing and pigment inks remain wet longer whereas dye inks dry almost immediately on most papers. The ink needs to remain wet long enough to apply the embossing powder. Second, you need an embossing powder. The type you use will depend on the look you want to achieve and the stamp image you wish to emboss. Finally, you need a heat tool. Unfortunately, a hair dryer will not work, since it will not get hot enough to melt the powder.

Marvy Heat Tool

There are four main types of embossing powder. Regular embossing powder is the most common. Using regular powder will give you good results with most stamp images.

Regular embossing powder sample.

Regular Embossing Powder

However, certain stamp images will look nicer using a more specialized powder. Detail powders are much finer and will work better for a stamp image that has a lot of detail.

Detail embossing powder sample.

Ranger Super Fine Detail Embossing Powder

Embossing enamels are great for bold images. They also add more dimension to your project.

Enamels embossing sample.

Ranger Ultra Thick Embossing Enamel

Finally, distress powders are designed to give an image an old, worn look, since some of the crystals are meant to be rubbed off after the image is embossed.

Distress embossing powder sample.

Ranger Distress Embossing Powder

All four samples show the same stamp used with each of these four types of powder.

The actual wet embossing technique is not difficult. Ink your image and stamp onto the paper. Sprinkle the embossing powder over the entire image and shake off excess powder. Pour any extra powder back into your container. Next, heat the image. Keep the heat tool 6–8 inches away from your paper and keep it moving while the powders are heating. Getting the heat tool too close to your paper or keeping it in one spot for too long may result in a burned image or a warped piece of paper. The heat tool should be handled very carefully. It can cause damage to the skin if not used properly. Once the powder reaches the correct temperature, after about 2–5 seconds, it will start to melt and your embossed image will appear.

Heat tool demonstration.

After mastering the basic technique, try taking your skills to the next level. Combine different colours of powder for a multicoloured embossed image. Or, add a small amount of glitter to your powder for an image that sparkles. Finally, rub ink directly across the top of a clear embossed

Resist embossing sample.

image for a unique look. This is known as a resist. After you have rubbed the ink over your embossed image, wipe it clean with a cotton ball.

The best part about wet embossing is that there are really no rules—the above information about powders and images are just basic guidelines. You can use different combinations of powders and images to achieve the desired look of your project.

Dry Embossing

Although the less common of the two embossing styles, dry embossing gives your projects as much class and elegance as wet embossing. It can be more tool intensive than wet embossing; however, it doesn't have to be expensive. There are some great low cost alternatives that can be used to achieve the same look.

Lightrace Lightbox

Fiskars Stylus

The basic tools required for dry embossing are a light box, an embossing tool or stylus and a stencil, typically made

of metal or brass. It is also helpful to have waxed paper and removable tape handy, although neither is required to complete the technique. To dry emboss an image, place the stencil on a light box. Then, place your paper on top of the stencil. Removable tape can be used to secure the stencil and the paper while embossing. Depending on the thickness and the colour of the paper you are using, you should be able to see the stencil through the paper. Run the embossing tool along the edges of the stencil image you wish to emboss. Keep in mind that if you are using a printed paper, you will want your print to be facing down. If you have difficulty rubbing your embossing tool around the paper, try rubbing the back of the paper with waxed paper before you emboss the image. This will give your paper a slicker surface.

Some substitutions can be made in order to avoid investing in some of the higher-priced tools required for dry embossing. Make your own light box by placing a lamp under a glass topped table. Or emboss without a light source by running your embossing tool over the entire stencil and embossing "blindly." You can also emboss images onto your paper using items other than embossing stencils. Try cutting shapes out of thin chipboard. Place these thick shapes under your

Brass stencils

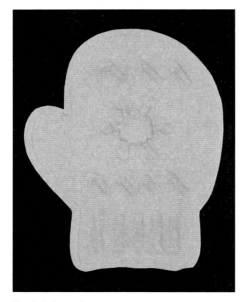

Simple look sample.

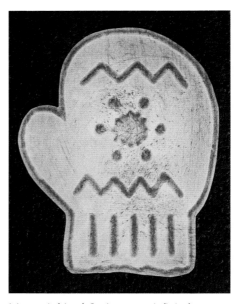

Inks sample (above). Sandpaper sample (below).

paper and emboss around the image. Or, find items from your garage, home or craft room that have interesting textures and emboss those textures onto your paper. Stone tiles, screen or mesh all have great textures. You can even skip using an embossing tool or stylus and use your fingers, a dried-out ball point pen or even sandpaper to emboss onto paper. Some thicker papers may not work as well with these alternative methods, so keep that in mind and try them out on scrap paper before using on your final project.

Once your image is embossed, you can leave it as is and use it on your project for an understated, simple look. You can add more interest by rubbing chalks, metallic rub-ons or inks onto the finished image. If your paper has a white core and is not a solid card stock, you can use sandpaper to remove some of the colour or patterning from your embossed image. This will give your project a great distressed look. Finally, consider embossing the same image in several different colours, cutting portions out and piecing them all together for a paper piecing with lots of dimension.

Whichever style of embossing you decide to try, be sure to experiment with different images, powders, inks and textures. You will be surprised at how versatile these two techniques can be—both styles of embossing may end up being used often for many of your future paper-craft projects. ■

Dimension sample.

Black Ribbon
Celebrate, page 102

Holly Leaf Votive Wrap, page 100

FROM THE HEART

Micro beads and heart-themed ribbon grace the edges of this Valentine gift box filled with tokens of your affection.

Design | Loretta Mateik

Materials
Small papier-mâché box with lid
White card stock
"From the Heart" rubber stamp
Watermark ink pad
Red embossing powder
Micro beads: red, clear
⅜-inch-wide hearts ribbon
Embossing heat tool
Paper crimper
½-inch-wide double-sided tape

Instructions
Stamp "From the Heart" on white card stock using watermark ink; sprinkle with red embossing powder and emboss. Using box lid as a template, cut out stamped message, centring it in heart.

Run a 1 x 11-inch strip white card stock through paper crimper. Starting at top centre of heart, adhere strip around box using double-sided tape, aligning edge of strip with bottom of box. Cut off any excess.

Adhere stamped heart to box lid using double-sided tape.

Wrap double-sided tape around top edge of lid so that about ⅛ inch is adhered to side and remaining tape protrudes evenly above top. Fold tape over onto top of lid, clipping as needed so tape lies flat. Peel off protective paper backing and cover tape with a mixture of red and clear micro beads.

Adhere ribbon around edges of lid using additional double-sided tape. Tie a small bow from a separate piece of ribbon; adhere to edge of lid at point. ■

From the Heart
Rubber stamp from Stampin' Up!; ink pad from Tsukineko Inc.

ALWAYS VALENTINE TAG

Embellish the front of a simple tag with wildly romantic items such as antique buttons and lace!

Design | Susan Stringfellow

Materials

Card stock: green, pink
Green printed paper
Vintage valentine image, approximately 4 x 2$\frac{7}{16}$ inches
"Always" sticker
Clear embossing ink pad
Metallic gold embossing powder
Vintage lace or tatted edging
2 Victorian-style buttons
Glass leaf beads
Gold butterfly pin
Decorative fibres: peach, green, gold
Embossing heat tool
¼-inch hole punch
Glue stick
Paper glaze

Instructions

Cut a 4½ x 3-inch piece of green printed paper; tear off bottom edge. Adhere to green card stock, using glue stick, and trim a small border; tear off bottom edge of card stock.

Fold a small piece of vintage lace or tatted edging to resemble a handkerchief; affix butterfly pin to lace. Adhere "handkerchief" to bottom left corner with paper glaze.

Cut out valentine image; tear off bottom edge. Rub edges of valentine image on embossing ink pad; sprinkle with gold embossing powder and emboss. Adhere valentine image to pink card stock with glue stick; trim a small border; tear pink card stock along bottom edge. Adhere pink tag to green tag at an angle with glue stick, overlapping handkerchief.

Attach "Always" sticker in upper left corner of tag. Adhere buttons and leaf beads above lace with paper glaze. Punch hole through top of tag; cut fibres 7–9 inches long and thread through hole. ■

Always Valentine Tag
Printed paper from Creative Imaginations;
vintage image from Altered Pages; sticker
from Starfish and Dreams; beads from Blue
Moon Beads; paper glaze from JudiKins.

EMBOSSED FLOWERS

Make this birthday card in minutes with some easy embossing and a dusting of chalk.

Design | Eileen Hull

Materials

Flower Patch white embossed card
Light blue mat board
Brass flower stencil
"Happy Birthday" rubber stamp
White ink pad
Turquoise chalk
2 light blue round beads
12 inches ¼-inch-wide blue gingham ribbon
2 silver jump rings
Sandpaper
Embossing tool
Stencil brush
Craft knife
¹⁄₁₆-inch hole punch
Paper glue

Instructions

Cut a 1¼-inch square and a 1¼ x 1-inch rectangle from mat board. Place stencil on top of square and use embossing tool to press flower design firmly into square. Brush white ink on top of embossed flower. Stamp "Happy Birthday" image onto rectangle. Sand edges of both. Punch two ¹⁄₁₆-inch holes through bottom edge of square and top edge of rectangle; use jump rings to attach pieces together as shown.

Brush turquoise chalk randomly onto embossed flowers on card. Cut a ¼-inch slit through card fold, two inches from top. Thread ribbon through slit; bring ribbon to front and string a bead on each side. Knot on left side; trim ribbon ends. Adhere mat board pieces to card as shown. ∎

Embossed Flowers
Embossed card from Die Cuts With A View; brass stencil and rubber stamp from Plaid Enterprises; Zip Dry Paper Glue from Beacon Adhesives Inc.

FALL PATCHWORK FRAME

Embossing powder makes the stamped leaves on this frame glow with all the brilliance of autumn trees.

Design | Sandra Graham Smith

Materials
8½ x 6⅝-inch flat frame with
   7 x 5-inch opening
Textured card stock: brown, green, rust, dark gold
Leaf rubber stamps
Clear embossing ink pad
Copper embossing powder
Embossing heat tool
Double-sided adhesive

Instructions
From each colour of card stock, cut several 1½-inch-long strips wide enough to cover frame. Alternating colours, adhere strips to frame using double-sided adhesive.

Cut three or four 1½-inch squares from each colour of card stock. Stamp a leaf onto each square using embossing ink pad; sprinkle with embossing powder and emboss.

Adhere embossed card-stock squares to frame, spacing them evenly and aligning outer edges of squares with outer edges of frame. Squares will overhang centre opening somewhat. ■

Fall Patchwork Frame
Card stock from Die Cuts With A View; stamps from Northwoods Rubber Stamps Inc.

HOLLY LEAF VOTIVE WRAP

Create festive lighting for your holiday event with this elegant votive wrap.

Design | Sharon Reinhart

Materials
Olive green iridescent paper
Gold vellum
Glass votive holder with candle
Rubber stamps: holly leaf, bow
Clear embossing ink pad
Gold embossing powder
Decorative-edge scissors
Embossing heat tool
Adhesive dots
Adhesive foam dots

Instructions
Stamp two holly leaves onto gold vellum using embossing ink; sprinkle with embossing powder and emboss. Repeat to stamp and emboss two holly leaves and two gift bows on olive green paper. Cut out embossed images.

Gently curl tips of holly leaves over edge of a scissors blade. Adhere leaves to back of one gift bow using adhesive dots, arranging gold leaves on the top and olive green leaves on the bottom.

On remaining gift bow image, lightly crease bow loops along each side of centre of bow; adhere on top of first bow using adhesive foam dots.

Cut a 2-inch-wide strip of gold vellum long enough to fit around votive candleholder with ½-inch overlap; trim ¼ inch from each long edge using decorative-edge scissors. Adhere strip around votive candleholder using adhesive dots. Adhere holly-and-bow piece over seam using adhesive dots. ■

Holly Leaf Votive Wrap
Rubber stamps from DeNami Design and
Delta Creative Inc./Rubber Stampede.

BLACK RIBBON CELEBRATE

Send Happy New Year wishes in a handmade card that sparkles and shines.

Design | Julie Ebersole

Materials

Card stock: ivory, black
Watercolour paper
Rubber stamps: champagne glasses, small star, "celebrate!," "Happy New Year"
Ivory envelope to fit a 5½ x 4¼-inch card
Pigment ink pads: black, metallic gold
Clear embossing powder
Gold water-based marker
Clear glaze pen
⅞-inch-wide black sheer ribbon
2 gold round brads
1/16-inch hole punch
Embossing heat tool
Adhesive foam dots
Glue stick

Instructions

With black ink, stamp champagne glasses and "celebrate!" onto a 2¾ x 2¾-inch piece of watercolour paper; emboss with clear embossing powder. Stamp stars around images with metallic gold ink. Colour champagne glasses with gold marker; apply a top coat with clear glaze pen for dimension; let dry.

Tear off bottom edge; adhere to black card stock; trim a ⅛-inch border along top and sides; tear off bottom edge, leaving an approximately ¼-inch border. Punch 1/16-inch holes through top corners of watercolour piece; insert brads.

Form a 5½ x 4¼-inch top-folded card from ivory card stock. Stamp "Happy New Year" on lower right corner with black ink and emboss. Wrap ribbon around card front and knot on right side; trim ribbon ends at an angle. Use foam dots to adhere assembled panel to left side of card as shown.

In the same manner as for card, stamp, emboss and colour champagne glasses and a few stars on lower left area of envelope. ■

Celebrate!

Happy New Year

Black Ribbon C
Rubber stamps from
clear glaze pen from

LEARN TO STITCH ON PAPER

Stitching gives paper-craft projects a homemade feel—it is like looking at your grandmother's embroidered pillows or snuggling under an old patchwork quilt.

By | Connie Petertonjes

Stitching on paper is a hot trend. Your projects will have a comfortable, well-loved look. Additionally, it can serve as an actual design element for your projects, adding dimension and texture while not adding bulk or weight.

Machine Stitching

Machine stitching is the quickest way to stitch on your projects. A sewing machine does not need to be an expensive one to give you beautiful results. Straight and zigzag stitches are the most common stitches used and both are found on the majority of machines. You can achieve many different looks with these two basic stitches by varying the length of the stitches. You can also use your machine to sew shapes onto your projects.

Every machine is different. Before you start sewing, first practice on scrap paper. The thread tension may need to be adjusted depending on the paper you are using. Consult your owner's manual for instructions. Avoid stitching on paper that has already been adhered to another piece.

Sew Crafty Mini Sewing Machine from Provo Craft.

Depending on the type of adhesive used, your needle may begin to stick, preventing your paper from properly advancing. It is best to keep the adhesive away from the areas you plan to stitch.

For straight or zigzag stitches, there are no special techniques to follow. Just put your paper under the foot and start sewing. For shapes, words or letters, you will need to do a little preparation. Use templates to draw shapes or draw them free-hand using a pencil. While stitching along those pencil lines, press the machine pedal slowly. It is best to do your shaped stitching at a slower pace. When you are done, you can erase any visible pencil marks. Finish your stitching with one of two methods.

Use a backstitch for a less polished look or pull the top thread through to the back of your project and tie in a double knot for a more finished look.

Hand Stitching

The possibilities are endless with hand stitching. Most embroidery stitches can be done on paper, as well as regular straight stitches. Hand stitching takes a little more preparation, but you can achieve a much different look with this type of sewing. Try stitching small flowers or other detailed shapes. These shapes are not easily achieved with a machine unless you have an expensive machine designed to embroider shapes and letters.

Use a pencil to draw the shape you wish to stitch. A backstitch is the most common stitch used for hand stitching, but feel free to experiment with other embroidery stitches. Practice on scrap paper until you get the feel for stitching on paper. Before sewing on your paper, poke the holes through which you will stitch. Hand stitching on paper is harder than on fabric since the paper is not as easily pierced. Poking your holes before stitching will assist you in getting the needle and thread through the paper without tearing it. Hand stitching is more time consuming than machine stitching, but with a little planning, you can have a wonderful, handmade piece ready to display or give as a gift.

Faux Stitching

Still not convinced you can machine or hand stitch on your paper-craft projects? Why not try faux stitching? You will achieve a similar look with less effort and in less time.

Use a marker or pen to draw stitch lines around an object on your project. Rub-on stitches are also available in a variety of colours and designs. Finally, many rubber stamp companies design stamps that mimic the look of machine or hand stitching.

Whatever type of stitching you decide to try on your paper-craft projects, definitely give one of these techniques a try. Stitching is a wonderful way of adding interest to your projects while still giving them a homemade feel. ■

"IF MOTHERS WERE FLOWERS" CARD

What better words to say to your mom? Let her know you'd choose her with this cheerful card embellished with rows of tiny buttons.

Design | Mary Ayres

Materials
Card stock: white, assorted pastel colours
Mini pastel buttons
Pink craft thread
Flower and leaf punches
Embroidery needle
Permanent fabric glue
Computer and printer (optional)

Instructions
Fold card stock to make card. Tear a square from white to fit front of card. Punch flowers from assorted pastel colours card stock and glue on white square in diagonal rows; sew a button in centre of each flower. Glue white square to front of card. Hand-print, or use a computer to generate, "If mothers were flowers" on pastel card stock and tear into strip; glue across top of card. Repeat with another colour of card stock, printing "I'd pick you" and tear into a strip to fit across bottom of card. Punch out a flower and two leaves from card stock; glue flower above "i" in "pick" and glue leaves beside flower. Sew a stitch across each leaf and sew button in centre of flower. Using photo as a guide, whipstitch across top and bottom edges of white square, overlapping strips and knotting ends on inside. ■

"If Mothers Were Flowers" Card
Mini pastel buttons from Karen Foster
Design; flower and leaf punches from
EK Success; Fabri-Tac Glue from Beacon
Adhesives Inc.

School Spirit Graduation Journal

Fill this tiny album with high school or college memories!

Design | Mary Ayres

Materials

6 x 9-inch wooden memory journal with window opening
Card stock: orange, white and navy or card stock in
   desired school colours
Bottle cap
School emblem image to fit onto bottle cap
4 x 6-inch graduation photo
Black fine-tip marker
12 silver mini round brads
8 silver photo corners
Silver pigment ink pad
1/16-inch hole punch
Sewing machine with silver thread
Paper glue
Computer and printer (optional)

Instructions

Rub silver ink onto front cover; let dry completely. Rub silver ink inside front cover; let dry completely.

Cut a 5 x 8-inch rectangle from orange card stock; referring to photo, cut a 4¼-inch square from top portion of card stock that will fit around journal opening. Glue orange piece to white card stock; trim a small border along inside and outside edges. Repeat with navy card stock.

Cut a 4¼ x 2⅝-inch rectangle from white card stock; glue symmetrically at bottom of layered piece. Cut a 4 x 2⅜-inch rectangle from navy card stock; draw an "x" through centre of rectangle, from corner to corner. Cut rectangle along lines, forming four triangles. Referring to photo, glue two larger triangles at top and bottom of white rectangle with points touching in centre.

Referring to photo, machine-stitch around edge of orange card stock, underneath opening and along triangle edges. Punch 1/16-inch holes in corners of white rectangle, in corners of opening and in corners of orange card stock; attach brads. Glue assembled piece to front of journal.

Glue school emblem onto bottle cap; adhere bottle cap to centre of navy triangles.

For inside front cover, cut a 5½ x 8½-inch rectangle from navy card stock; cut a 3¾-inch square opening to fit around journal opening. Glue piece inside front cover.

Layer a 5 x 8-inch piece of orange card stock onto navy card stock; trim edges, leaving a small border. Glue to first journal page. Place silver photo corners on photo; centre and glue toward top portion of layered rectangles.

Hand-print, or use a computer to generate, a congratulatory sentiment onto white card stock; trim a rectangle around sentiment. Place silver photo corners on rectangle and glue onto navy card stock. Trim a small border. Glue below photo. ■

School Spirit Graduation Journal
Wooden memory journal from Walnut
Hollow; bottle cap from Li'l Davis Designs.

GIFT BAG

*Zigzag stitching adds to the charm
of this handmade gift bag.*

Design | Melony Bradley

Materials

5¼ x 8½-inch plain gift bag
Double-sided printed papers: Gazebo Paisley, Scarlet
    Polka Dots
Chalk ink: dark brown, lipstick red
20 inches 1-inch-wide turquoise grosgrain ribbon
2½-inch tag punch
¾-inch paper flower
2 turquoise mini brads
Alphabet rub-on transfers
Brown all-purpose thread
Paper trimmer
Hand-sewing needle
Hole punch
Sewing machine
Paper glue

Instructions

Carefully remove handles from bag. Cut turquoise ribbon
into two 10-inch lengths. Hand-sew ends to interior sides
at top of bag.

Cut two 2¼ x 5¼-inch pieces from each sheet of printed
paper. Ink all edges with dark brown ink. Alternate solid
and printed sides of paper and adhere together with paper
glue, overlapping papers ¼-inch each.

Using a sewing machine, zigzag-stitch across paper
"seams" as shown. Adhere sewn piece to front of bag with
paper glue.

Punch tag from scrap of Scarlet Polka Dots printed paper.
Ink edges with dark brown ink.

Cut solid side of Gazebo Paisley printed paper to 1½ x
2 inches. Ink edges with lipstick red ink and adhere to
centre of tag. Ink edges of paper flower with lipstick red
ink. Insert brad in flower centre and adhere to top left of
tag. Using sewing machine, straight-stitch edge of tag,
continuing across silk flower.

Use rub-on transfers to spell "a gift" in centre of tag.
Punch hole in centre top of tag. Insert remaining brad
through hole and glue tag to bag. ■

Gift Bag
Gazebo Paisley and Scarlet Polka Dots printed paper from Chatterbox Inc.; alphabet rub-on transfers from Making Memories; chalk ink from Clearsnap Inc.; Zip Dry paper glue from Beacon Adhesives Inc.

FLOWER BLOOM TRAY

A single paper flower gets all the attention with this paper-accented serving tray.

Design | Kelly Anne Grundhauser

Materials

12½ x 12½-inch white wooden serving tray with removable bottom
White card stock
Textured card stock: brown, aqua, green
Aqua floral printed paper
Ribbon scraps
Brown ink pad
Sandpaper
Sewing machine with brown thread
Repositionable adhesive
Craft glue

Instructions

Project note: *To use tray for serving, protect card-stock mat with glass or Plexiglas, or apply a waterproof decoupage to mat following manufacturer's instructions.*

Cut a total of 30 (2-inch) squares from white, green and aqua textured card stock and printed paper. Place a small amount of repositionable adhesive on back of each square and lay out on brown textured card stock, spacing so brown shows through to create five more 2-inch squares.

Using a wide zigzag stitch, stitch across edges of squares in vertical and horizontal rows. If desired, stitch horizontal rows without thread in an alternating zigzag pattern to add texture without thickness.

Remove bottom from tray. Line tray bottom with stitched card-stock mat, trimming edges even, if needed. Glue in place with craft glue; replace tray bottom.

Cut eight 3½-inch petals from white card stock; ink edges. When dry, arrange petals to form a flower in one corner of tray; glue in place with craft glue.

Cut a circle from brown card stock. Using a straight stitch, stitch inside centre of circle and sand lightly to add texture. Glue circle over ends of petals in centre of flower. Knot scraps of ribbon over tray handles. ∎

PERFUME BOTTLE CARD

Create an elegant card with the image of a vintage perfume bottle, then tuck it into a stitched vellum envelope tied with pink ribbon for a unique finishing touch!

Design | Mary Ayres

Materials

Card stock: brown, pale yellow, sage green
Vintage floral printed paper
Pink iridescent paper
Pink mulberry paper
Vellum
Cork sheet
⅛-inch-wide silk ribbon
White dye ink pad
Black fine-tip marker
⅛-inch brass eyelets with eyelet setter
⅛-inch hole punch
Pinking shears
Sewing machine with white thread
Permanent fabric glue
Computer and printer (optional)

Card

Fold pale yellow card stock in half for card; glue a torn rectangle of brown card stock to front. Use provided pattern to tear a bottle shape from vellum, then lightly press stamp pad randomly on bottle to create texture. Cut rectangle from vintage floral print paper; tear a rectangle from pink mulberry paper to fit behind floral print and glue mulberry-backed print to front of bottle. Machine-stitch around edges of floral print. Cut cork sheet for stopper and glue to top back of bottle; glue a length of ribbon to back of stopper with ends extended evenly, then glue assembled bottle to front of card. Machine-stitch around side and bottom edges of bottle, and around edges of brown rectangle.

Hand-print, or use a computer to generate, "Happy Mother's Day" on sage green card stock; trim to make tag; back with pink iridescent paper trimmed with pinking shears. Punch hole in end of tag and set eyelet. Slip ribbon through eyelet and tie ends in bow.

Envelope

Tear two rectangles from vellum slightly larger than card size; add texture with white stamp pad as for bottle. Place rectangles together and punch two holes through centre top of both layers 1½ inches apart; separate rectangles and set eyelets. Machine-stitch rectangles together along side and bottom edges. Place card in envelope; insert a length of ribbon through eyelets and tie ends in a bow to close. ■

Perfume Bottle Card

Floral printed paper and pink iridescent paper from K&Company; Fabri-Tac Glue from Beacon Adhesives Inc.

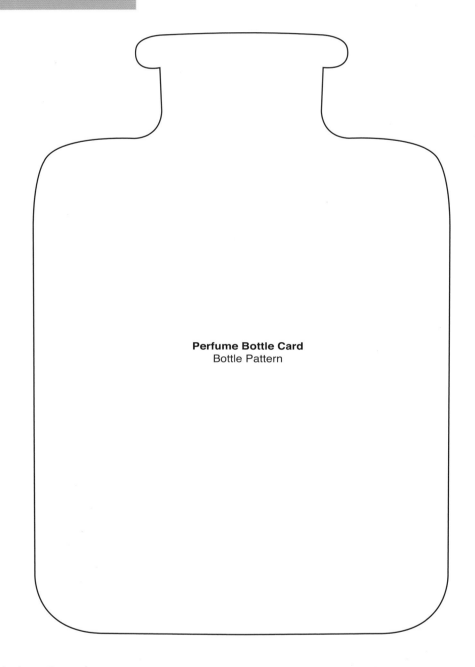

Perfume Bottle Card
Bottle Pattern

HALLOWEEN PAPER QUILT

The time-honoured craft of quilting carries over into paper with this whimsical wall quilt. Odds and ends from your craft stash make this a one-of-a-kind creation.

Design | Mary Ayres

Materials

⅜-inch-diameter wooden dowel
2 (12-inch) squares grey card stock
Printed papers: 9 assorted designs
Handmade papers: yellow, orange
2½ x 1½-inch tea-dyed tag
3½-inch-square walnut watermarks slide mount
Vintage Halloween images
Victorian-style "H"
Photo
Ink pads: purple, brown, gold
Black stain
Craft paints: gold metallic, orange
16 flat buttons
2 metal bookplates
Mini brads: 4 gold, 4 silver
Round copper letters to spell "BOO"
Gold eyelet and eyelet-setting tool
1½-inch gold key
1-inch round metal frame
Silver metal hinge
1½ x 1⅞-inch maple leaf plaque
4-inch green zipper
Gauze fabric
Tan splattered adhesive net
Black hemp cord
⅜-inch-wide black striped ribbon
Yellow coloured pencil
Black fine-tip marker

Small dry sponge
⅛-inch hole punch
Paintbrushes
Pinking shears
Sewing machine with black thread
Paper glue
Computer and printer (optional)

Instructions

Using dry sponge, rub edges of one sheet grey card stock with purple ink. Using a ruler and pencil, divide sheet into nine 4-inch squares. Using a straight stitch, machine-stitch over lines; adhere thread ends on back. Adhere second sheet of grey card stock to back of stitched square.

Cut quilt block motif from each of nine printed papers; ink edges purple. Adhere shapes in squares on card stock with points in corners. Glue buttons to corners of squares.

Using patterns provided, embellish squares, adhering embellishments.

Top left: Adhere pumpkin image over gauze fabric.

Top centre: Using black stain, antique metal bookplates. Hand-print, or use a computer to generate, "happy" and "haunting" on card stock; insert in bookplates. Use gold mini brads to adhere bookplates to quilt.

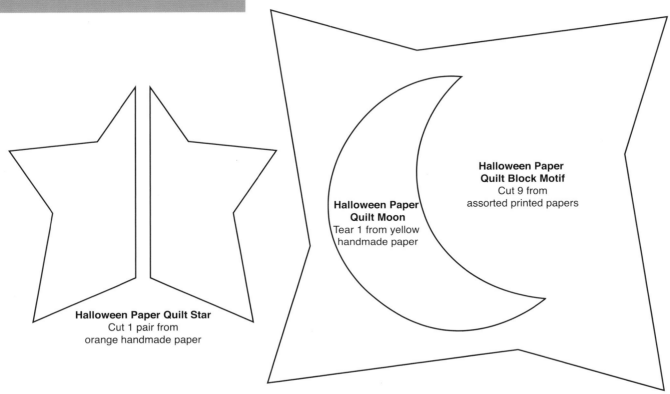

Halloween Paper Quilt Star
Cut 1 pair from
orange handmade paper

**Halloween Paper
Quilt Moon**
Tear 1 from yellow
handmade paper

**Halloween Paper
Quilt Block Motif**
Cut 9 from
assorted printed papers

Top right: Adhere copper alphabet letters to spell "BOO" to tea-dyed tag; add eyelet and hemp cord bow.

Centre left: Rub edges of zipper with purple ink; tie on key using hemp cord.

Centre centre: Adhere photo behind slide mount.

Centre right: Tear moon from yellow handmade paper; rub edges with gold ink. Adhere cat image.

Bottom left: Rub edges of Victorian "H" with brown ink. Adhere round frame; using yellow pencil, colour area inside frame.

Bottom centre: Cut star halves from orange handmade paper; ink edges gold. Antique hinge using black stain; adhere over star halves using silver mini brads.

Bottom right: Dry-brush leaf plaque with orange paint; adhere over tan splattered adhesive net.

Paint dowel gold. Cut four 3½-inch pieces of ribbon; fold each into loop. Glue 1 inch of ribbon ends across top back edge of paper quilt; insert dowel through loops. ■

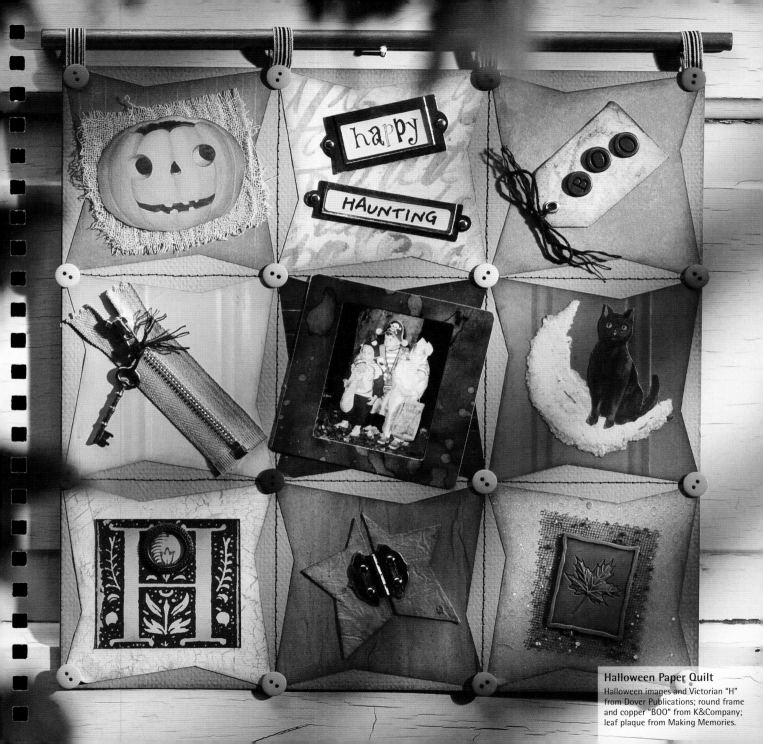

Halloween Paper Quilt
Halloween images and Victorian "H"
from Dover Publications; round frame
and copper "BOO" from K&Company;
leaf plaque from Making Memories.

CHRISTMAS TREE GIFT SET

Buttons and wool felt add dimension to this quick-and-easy coordinating candle and gift-card set.

Designs | Mary Ayres

Materials

6-inch ivory pillar candle
Red card stock
Green wool felt
Flat buttons: 3 (½-inch), 3 (⅝-inch)
Cinnamon sticks
⅛-inch-wide wire-edge metallic gold ribbon
Ivory pearl cotton or embroidery floss
2 gold eyelets and eyelet setter
Texturizing plate
Embossing tool
³⁄₁₆-inch hole punch
Embroidery needle
Sewing machine with metallic gold thread
Permanent fabric glue

Candle

Using patterns provided, cut candle tag from red card stock and candle tree from wool felt. Emboss vertical lines on tag using texturizing plate and embossing tool. Thread sewing machine with metallic gold thread; machine-stitch around tag ⅛ inch from edge. Punch ³⁄₁₆-inch hole in top of tag; set eyelet in hole.

Adhere felt tree to tag. Using embroidery needle, poke holes through tree and tag as shown by dots on pattern. Stitching through holes, work blanket stitch around edge of felt tree using embroidery needle and one strand ivory

pearl cotton (or three plies separated from a strand of embroidery floss); adhere knots on back.

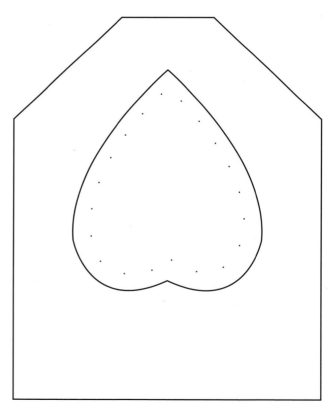

Christmas Tree Gift Set Candle Tag
Cut tag from red card stock;
cut tree from green wool felt

Christmas Tree Gift Set
Embossing tool from Fiskars; Fabri-Tac
Glue from Beacon Adhesives Inc.

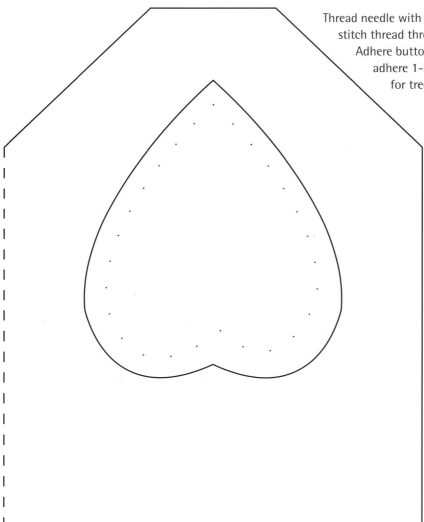

Christmas Tree Gift Set Card
Make card from red card stock;
cut tree from green wool felt

Thread needle with several strands of metallic gold thread; stitch thread through buttons, knotting ends on front. Adhere buttons to tree using permanent adhesive; adhere 1-inch piece of cinnamon stick to tag for tree trunk.

Position centre of ribbon on back of tree near top; bring ends around candle and through eyelet in tag from back to front; take ribbons down and around to back of candle; knot ends tightly. Wrap a second piece of ribbon around candle, tying ends in a bow over cinnamon stick. Secure ribbons with permanent glue.

Card

Referring to instructions for candle and using patterns provided for card, cut tag-shaped card from folded red card stock, positioning dashed line on fold. Emboss front of card and machine-stitch around edges. Add tree and eyelet to front of card, using ⅝-inch buttons and a 1½-inch piece of cinnamon stick. Glue bow of gold ribbon to front of card over tree trunk. ■

INDEX

INDEX

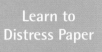

INDEX

METRIC CONVERSION CHARTS

		METRIC CONVERSIONS	
yards	x	.9144	= metres (m)
yards	x	91.44	= centimetres (cm)
inches	x	2.54	= centimetres (cm)
inches	x	25.40	= millimetres (mm)
inches	x	.0254	= metres (m)

centimetres	x	.3937	= inches
metres	x	1.0936	= yards

INCHES INTO MILLIMETRES & CENTIMETRES (Rounded off slightly)

inches	mm	cm	inches	cm	inches	cm	inches	cm
1/8	3	0.3	5	12.5	21	53.5	38	96.5
1/4	6	0.6	5 1/2	14	22	56	39	99
3/8	10	1	6	15	23	58.5	40	101.5
1/2	13	1.3	7	18	24	61	41	104
5/8	15	1.5	8	20.5	25	63.5	42	106.5
3/4	20	2	9	23	26	66	43	109
7/8	22	2.2	10	25.5	27	68.5	44	112
1	25	2.5	11	28	28	71	45	114.5
1 1/4	32	3.2	12	30.5	29	73.5	46	117
1 1/2	38	3.8	13	33	30	76	47	119.5
1 3/4	45	4.5	14	35.5	31	79	48	122
2	50	5	15	38	32	81.5	49	124.5
2 1/2	65	6.5	16	40.5	33	84	50	127
3	75	7.5	17	43	34	86.5		
3 1/2	90	9	18	46	35	89		
4	100	10	19	48.5	36	91.5		
4 1/2	115	11.5	20	51	37	94		

We have a sweet lineup of cookbooks with plenty more in the oven

www.companyscoming.com